AF405336

SUSPENSE
TWELVE YEARS
LIVING AND LONGING
ON DEATH ROW

Marit Lund Bødtker

SUSPENSE
TWELVE YEARS
LIVING AND LONGING
ON DEATH ROW

Translated from
the Norwegian
by J. Basil Cowlishaw

© 2017 Yuniku Publishing
2nd edition 2018
CreateSpace, Seattle, USA
978-8293522102 (Paperback edition)
Original title in Norwegian:
Dødsdømt 989. Manifest 2014.
Cover layout: Fiverr
Other illustrations: Ivan Ray Murhphy Jr. and
Emilio Nathaniel Taveras

For Jan Kristian, Joakim and Silje

CONTENTS

HOW IT ALL BEGAN

2014

I had been busy dusting. For weeks and months I had been going through piles of old papers: copies of more than a hundred letters to him and even more from him. There were also notes I had made, newspaper cuttings and other relevant documents – a thousand or so pages in all. I had tidied them up, numbered them, punched holes in them and filed them in the right order in three large, meticulously labelled binders. I had thought, pondered, made copious notes and talked to anyone who would listen.

Almost without exception, whenever I spoke of this somewhat unusual relationship, I was asked: 'What exactly had he done?' It often seemed that what people really wanted to know was whether his sentence was justified. Rarely did a meaningful conversation ensue. As a rule, the person concerned hurriedly changed the subject. Capital punishment is far from being a pleasant topic of conversation and is hardly a subject for social chit-chat. That is why it deserves closer consideration.

1993

In its 1993 news bulletin, the Norwegian branch of
Amnesty International appealed to members to write
to prisoners in what the organization referred to as
Death's Waiting Room, that is, Death Row in the State
Penitentiary at Huntsville, Texas. Apart from a brief
note pointing out that most of the inmates were
destitute, no more information was given. This
notwithstanding, my journalistic curiosity was aroused
and I phoned in to express my interest.

I had no inkling of what I was letting myself in
for until, a few weeks later, I received a letter from
Amnesty with which was enclosed a brief handwritten
letter from one Ivan Ray Murphy Jr, Prisoner No.
989.

In a few short sentences he told me something
about himself. Twenty-eight years of age, he was
under sentence of death and had spent two and a half
years in a cell at the Penitentiary's Ellis Unit 1 in
Huntsville; prior to that, he had served close on five
years behind bars elsewhere. His mother was a full-
blooded Cherokee Indian, his father an Irishman. He
said he had blue eyes, dark-brown hair, was by nature
shy and retiring, polite, caring, serious-minded and
loyal to a fault. He also said that he was fond of
drawing, chess, reading and composing poetry and
that he was a prolific letter-writer. In the past he had
been a keen fisherman but, as he wryly pointed out,
that was a pleasure now denied him.

He concluded by saying:

> I would like to hear from honest open- minded
> people between the age (sic) of 25 to 60 that
> wants an honest loyal lasting friend.

Ivan's letter to Amnesty Norway was dated 22 June
1993, which meant that it had taken two months to
reach me. I dug out an old postcard depicting a typical
fishing boat from Norway's Lofoten Islands, with a
member of the crew holding in his arms a giant cod.
On it I promised to write again, more fully, before
long. As a precaution, I put the card in an envelope.
Amnesty had warned me that all letters to prisoners
were subject to censorship but that the prisoners' own
letters were not. Ivan spent his days in a cell
measuring three by three metres. I just hoped he
would find somewhere on the wall to put up the card.

I read and reread the letter from Amnesty that
had accompanied Ivan's brief reply. It read in
translation:

> Incarcerated in Ellis Unit [the official name of
> the prison] are a small number of the men
> currently under sentence of death in the
> United States. The prison, which stands in a
> wide expanse of open country, houses a total
> of 1,900 prisoners, all of them men. Prisoners
> not condemned to death are regularly engaged
> in agricultural work outside the prison. The
> large, three-storey-high, red-brick building is

surrounded by watch towers and barriers of various kinds. Prisoners under sentence of death are allowed to mix only with others in the same situation and the prison guards. Each cell is fitted with a steel wash basin and a toilet bowl. Some prisoners, those who are subject to an extra-rigorous security regime, have their meals passed to them through a hatch in the door. Rules are extremely strict. Prisoners have no privacy, not even when showering or using the toilet. They wear white overalls complete with orange name tags and receive regular meals and medical care. Minor ailments are attended to by the unit's own doctor. Prisoners consider themselves fortunate if they are deemed so ill as to necessitate treatment in the nearest town, Galveston, as this enables them to catch a glimpse of the outside world from the windows of the ambulance.

I simply couldn't wait. My curiosity triumphed over my uncertainty as to what this might lead to. My mind made up, I sat down to compose my first letter to Ivan. Two weeks later, in August 1993, I posted it.

In my letter I told him that I was fifty-two years of age, that my husband's name was Eivind and that I had a son and a two-year-old Norwegian-American grandson. I also informed him that I had been a librarian but was currently a journalist and that I had published several books.

I concluded by saying that I hoped we could become friends and that my letters would help to brighten his daily life a little.

I also told him that I had always been strongly opposed to capital punishment, regardless of what a person had done, and that fortunately I lived in a country where it had long been abolished.

What I was careful not to say was that, as a journalist, I was intensely curious to know more about his life, and that I saw our budding friendship as a unique opportunity to learn more about what goes on within the confines of a prison; also, that one day I might be able to bring something of what I had learned to the notice of a wider public.

THE FIRST LETTER

I realized that it would be ten days at best before I could expect an answer – assuming that he replied at all. I did my best to put him out of my mind, but in vain; after all, never before had I been remotely associated with someone under sentence of death. Would I be able to control my own feelings? My prejudices? Although I had entered into the relationship with open eyes, I did not relish the thought that he might have been guilty of a sex crime or even of a multiple killing, not to mention incest or the murder of a child.

'People of this kind are looked upon as the dregs of society,' Amnesty had written. 'Accordingly, one must never let them down once one has started to correspond with them.'

I began to wonder whether I would be able to carry on without disappointing him.

After two suspenseful weeks, early in September 1993 I received my first letter from Ivan. Dated 31 August, it came in a long envelope and was handwritten in red ink on both sides of a sheet of lined yellow paper. Although I was the one who had taken the initiative, it nevertheless gave me a strange feeling to be holding it in my hand.

Dearest Marit,
Hello, I hope this letter finds you in the best of health and doing fine when it reaches your lovely hands. As for myself, I'm in good health and doing fine.

All Ivan's subsequent letters began with more or less the same words. The letter continued:

Your most welcome letter just reached my hands and I was very happy to receive it. I had 2 pen-pals from Norway at one time but I helped them with essays in school concerning the death penalty and after that I never heard from them again. So I had decided to write Amnesty again wanting an older friend that can be caring and loving as well as understanding. I set high standards for myself and follow them. As you get to know me you will know that I'm very caring and lovable and stand by my friends.

I will always be straightforward, honest and open-minded with you. There isn't anything too personal for me so feel free to ask all the questions your heart desires.

My days are somewhat boring. I get to go out and exercise 3 hours a day except on week-ends, then I'm locked in a cell 24 hours. I'm in a cell by myself. Before I leave my cell I have to strip naked and have to strip before being placed back in my cell. Breakfast is served at 3 AM, lunch is served at 9.30 AM and dinner is served at 2.30 PM and the food isn't fit for a dog. I don't have any outside

support, so I have to draw to obtain the basics
I need and most times I do without because
my art work doesn't always sell. When I get on
my feet I'll send you a sample of my art work
to give you some idea of the art work I do.
Marit, I hope to hear from you soon and
would like to know more about you. I'm
enclosing a photo of me with this letter that
was taken Christmas Day 1988, the last photo
taken of me in the free world. I would like
some photos of you. Thank you for taking the
time and think about me. I loved to go fishing.
You take care, stay sweet and write soon.
Love, Yours truly
Ivan Ray

The colour photograph enclosed with the letter was of
a slim, good-looking, smiling young man sitting on the
floor looking at a large, unopened Christmas present.
His dark hair was drawn back behind his ears and on
his head was a white baseball cap. He had a dark
moustache, dark eyebrows and blue eyes. He was
wearing a white T-shirt imprinted with some kind of
emblem in red, jeans and trainers. I noticed that the
trainers were spotlessly clean. Sitting beside him in an
old-fashioned armchair was a young woman, a
cigarette held between her fingers. Was she his sister, I
wondered, or his girlfriend? I had no means of
knowing, as he said nothing about her.
Ivan's early letters were long and full of enthusiasm,
though I couldn't help wondering if he was mildly
dyslectic: he invariably wrote 'grils' instead of 'girls',
for example.

The first and only photo Ivan ('Pee-Wee') ever sent.

To make for easier reading, in the following pages I have done my best to 'tidy up' his spelling, though not the grammar. Dyslectic or not, he had a rich vocabulary and I was pleased to observe how reflective and knowledgeable he was. He was keen to tell me all about himself and would write about all sorts of things, apart from his trial and sentence:

> About my case, I cannot write about it in a letter on the advice from my attorney because my case is still pending. But when I'm allowed to, I'll tell you everything about it. I can tell you this much, I am innocent of Murder and Robbery that I was convicted of and there is *no* evidence linking me to this crime, NONE!

For my part I was careful never to ask about either the trial or his sentence, though naturally I was curious. Amnesty had advised correspondents to avoid sensitive subjects unless the prisoner himself brought them up. Ivan was clearly reluctant or unable to bring himself to discuss such matters, at least not at this point. This notwithstanding, in one of his very first letters he had no compunction in telling me how he had felt when sentence was pronounced.

> Sure, I got disappointed when I received the death sentence and had no-one to talk to but myself, but being disappointed turned into negative thoughts, which only made my situation more difficult to handle. I have learned to love myself and others as well. I talk to very few people here. I have no friends, I try not to get too close to anyone here, for reasons that put me on death row.
>
> Do you know what is the worst by sitting here in the cell, Marit? Never to get the smell of soil and grass. I have not set foot on green grass for five years.
>
> I remember once I went to the lake at the big forest. When I was there, I felt the power of the old trees. I now know that's why I was so happy just then. The big trees give us my energy and beauty. Did you know, by the way, that we humans also provide forest and plants power? The deep forest likes us to visit it, it wants our attention.

To start with, we both wrote up to three letters a month, but the early ones were very hesitant and faltering. It was as if neither of us really believed that, in view of our socially different backgrounds, we could ever meet on the same plane. I asked him to tell me precisely what he expected of me and made it clear that I could not be of any practical assistance. I also pointed out that, although I was by no means impoverished, I was far from being rich. Amnesty had actually warned me that most prisoners were poor in the extreme and looked upon everyone in the outside world as millionaires. I did, however, offer to pay for his notepaper and stamps.

> I don't have anyone that I consider a friend, but, I feel that you and I will become very close friends. [. . .] People have told me many times that I have charisma like they have never seen before. They say my eyes take them away into a trance. Anyway, I don't get the big head whenever people tell me that.

We both endeavoured to get to know each other better by writing about everything imaginable – apart from what he had done to merit a death sentence. In one of his first letters Ivan asked me a string of questions, even going to the trouble of numbering them. One thing he wanted to know was what I liked most and least in life. I told him that my greatest joy was sitting with my little grandson on my lap when,

once a year, he and his parents came on a visit to
Norway. What I disliked, I said, were dishonesty,
disorder and selfishness. He also asked about my daily
life, about where I had been, what I had done, that
kind of thing. And he begged for photographs -- of me
and my family and of Norwegian scenery. 'I want to
know all about you,' he said.

He went on to ask what I expected of him. I
answered that most of all I was looking for a friend
with whom I could share my innermost thoughts.

I told him a great deal about myself: about my
friends, family, parents, habits (good and bad), joys,
sorrows and disappointments. But I asked him
questions, too. One of them was about his cell and
how it was decorated. He replied in detail:

> I have two beds, a top and bottom. At the
> back of my cell there is a toilet and sink. I have
> a calendar on the wall, that way all I have to
> do is turn around while I'm writing and mark
> your name on the day/date I mailed my letter
> to you. I have a locker box sitting against the
> wall. I'm allowed to watch TV and can listen
> to a radio if I had one to listen to. I have to
> buy those luxuries if I want them. [...] My
> favorite color is blue. I like shrimp, fish, all
> vegetables.
>
> Dream to be a singer and have lots of
> money to help children in need of the basics in
> life.

On one occasion I asked him if he thought I was being too inquisitive, too nosey. He assured me that I could ask him anything I liked and that he would give me a straight answer. No question was too big or too small, he said. The staff at Amnesty had told me the same thing: one could write all that was happening around one, about nature, holidays, excursions, it didn't matter what it was. Every little thing was of interest.

Ivan wrote that he hoped one day to be able to meet me in person, as a free man. He also expressed the hope that he would meet an attractive, kind-hearted woman whom he could marry and with whom he could have many children.

One day I received a letter with which he had enclosed a dainty little handkerchief. On it he had drawn two peacocks, one of them burgundy coloured. He knew from our previous correspondence that that was my favourite colour.

My first reaction, though I never said as much, was to wonder how someone who could draw so beautifully could have done something so terrible as to deserve the death penalty.

Copy from the handkerchief

FRIENDSHIP

Ivan told me that he not only drew, he also wrote poetry. My curiosity aroused, I urged him to share his poems with me.

The first poem I received from him was written after his arrest but two months before he was sentenced to death in 1990 and transferred to Death Row at Huntsville. It was highly revealing of the troubled life he had led.

The Devil You Know
When I was twelve I thought
Life was tough
When I was thirteen I had enough
I ran away from all my friends
unaware of life's little bends
it was good for a while to be on my own
until I was hungry cold and alone
I look back now and wonder why
Why did I leave and why do I cry?
But, I guess I found out too late
I wonder sometimes how I would have turned out
handsome, skilled and happy, no doubt
I wish I'd put up with that little pain
As that little makes this lot insane

I found it impossible to picture his day-to-day life. Whenever I sent him a postcard or photographs of myself and my family, I always tried to find some that were rich in background minutiae, as I knew that he spent a great deal of time studying them. I envied him his ability to describe small details in the pictures I sent him. He even contrived to imbue with a soul a plastic bin bag washed up on a beach, so finely honed had his critical faculties become in his enforced solitude.

For most of the time Ivan was indeed alone with his thoughts in the confines of his cell, but for three hours each day he was allowed out for a break. This brief period of relative freedom was very precious to him and he always put it to good purpose. There was a limited range of leisure-time activities open to prisoners in Ivan's position. They were at liberty to indulge in handicrafts of various kinds, were given facilities for study and had access to books. Ivan told me that he did a lot of reading. Prisoners not under sentence of death had a wider range of activities to choose from.

26

When, on rare occasions, he received a visitor from outside the prison, Ivan was taken in handcuffs to the Visiting Room, where he was ushered into what was little more than a cage and the handcuffs were removed.

Ivan had long dreamed of becoming a singer and nurtured the hope that one day he would be able to earn enough money to enable him to help youngsters in need. He told me that his favourite band was Journey and that he was a fan of country singers Garth Brooks and Tim McGraw. His favourite songs were the former's 'The Dance' and 'If Tomorrow Never Comes'. To gain an idea of what they were like, I went out and bought a selection of CDs.

With each letter I learned something new about him. It transpired that in his youth he had become addicted to both drugs and alcohol, but he assured me that all that lay far back in the past. He was now into meditation and meditated for two hours every day. It was one of the first things he confided in me, and he repeatedly emphasized how much it meant to him. He insisted that meditation had made him into a better person.

> I practice Siddha yoga. It's a meditation
> course and I have been taking the course for 1
> year and 3 months now. I have found the truth
> within myself. I had problems changing how
> my mind thinks but now that I know how the
> mind is I am a much better person. The ego is
> hard to change but once I seen that

everything is always the play of divine consciousness, I began to understand the basic truth. [. . .]

Ninety percent of a person's experience and perception during the day is in his/her imagination only, although he/she sincerely believes that what he/she imagines is due to the actions and words of others.

He also told me that to his family and friends he was known as Pee-Wee, the reason being that when he was born he had been the smallest baby in the Maternity Ward. He was adamant that there was nothing small about him at all, but that he liked the name and had kept it. Another reason for retaining his childhood nickname was that his father, Murphy Sr, bore the same first names, Ivan Ray, as himself. In time I too began to call him Pee-Wee.

I always received a prompt reply to my letters. An accomplished letter-writer, he displayed a rare warmth and evinced great interest in me and my everyday life while at the same time sharing with me the little that happened within the confines of his cell. He was especially interested in my relations with my mother and asked after her in every letter he wrote.

About this time my mother was beginning to show signs of approaching dementia. Prior to her admission to a nursing home, she would ring me as often as five times a day just to chat. When I confessed my annoyance at these repeated interruptions, Pee-

Wee gently chided me by pointing out that it was my
duty as a devoted daughter to humour her:

> I am happy that you get along better with your
> mother now. I think that she is just a lonely old
> lady that would like to have company and I
> am sure she doesn't annoy you on purpose. I
> wish I could just get a visit from my mother
> but I know she isn't 100% healthy and that is
> one of her reasons for not being able to make
> the trip down here. I would like to see my
> father too, I haven't seen him in a very long
> time. I know he doesn't like these places.

Although Pee-Wee was adept at handing out good
advice, he seldom complained about his own plight.
An exception was the summer when the temperature
in his cell soared to an unbearable 40 degrees C (104
degrees F):

> The weather hasn't cooled off much lately, I
> have no fan so I have had to endure the Texas
> heat. It doesn't really matter to me. People
> who lived 300 years ago on this earth didn't
> have fans or air conditioners either.

Prisoners were given nothing to drink after dinner,
which was at three in the afternoon. In desperation, at
night Pee-Wee slept on the floor of his cell, which
helped to alleviate his sufferings. He also slept with a
wet towel around his neck to help him keep cool.

Thinking it might interest him, I sent him a newspaper
cutting about a zoo in India where the keepers were
wont to place large blocks of ice in the animals' cages
to keep them cool. 'There's nothing like that here,'
was his laconic reply. 'Wild beasts are treated better
than we are.'

One day, quite out of the blue, he wrote that he was in
love with me. I realized at once that it was by no
means an unusual reaction. I had read and heard that
many prisoners fell deeply in love with their
correspondents and friends in the outside world, and
that sometimes their feelings were reciprocated. His
letter continued:

> I only get maybe two letters from you in a
> month and I don't complain about that at all.
> [. . .] I haven't heard from you in a long time.
> Have I said something that offended you.
> I don't know your true feelings towards me
> and how you see me through the window of
> your heart, but I would love to know.

Apart from the guards, he had not been in physical
contact with a free human being for several years. In
the prison it was strictly against the rules to initiate
personal relations with another prisoner or even to
give someone a friendly pat on the shoulder. I
understood his need to express his feelings but I found
it rather embarrassing and had to insist that he kept
them to himself.

To my relief, from then on he did. Instead, we began to discuss serious aspects of life and death and how he would face death should the worst come to the worst. In response, he told me about the many men he had tried to comfort before bidding them a last farewell on their transfer to The Walls, where those scheduled for execution spent their last hours before being given a lethal injection.

To me, our friendship was like a jigsaw puzzle, a puzzle that was destined to take years to complete. Slowly, a little at a time, we began to piece it together. There was hardly anything we didn't discuss: nothing was too important or too trifling.

In time, reading Pee-Wee's letters became one of the highlights of my day. He wanted to know where I sat when I read them, how many times I read them and what I liked most about them:

> I live a boring life but I have done a lot. Have you ever thought of writing a book about me?

He had given me something to think about. I began to view our relationship as a unique opportunity to do just that – but also as an almost insurmountable task. In reply, I thanked him for his faith in me, but said that I couldn't promise anything.

In due time Pee-Wee began to air a few philosophical observations. I can't say that I understood them all, but I did at least read his letters over and over again and do my best to follow his train of thought.

I resolved to keep an open mind with regard to what he had to say and never to judge him. I was amazed to discover how open one can be in writing, as opposed to when one is actually facing a person. I was also impressed by the fact that he could write so profoundly about life and mundane day-to-day happenings, and what was going on around him, when his own life was so circumscribed and he was confined to a cramped steel cage, faced with the knowledge that he might never leave it alive. It troubled me that I was able to live a normal life while he remained securely locked up behind bars.

The one thing he had that I didn't was time. This was a subject we were to discuss in depth in the years to come. Quite often, when I wrote him a letter, I would receive two or three in reply before I was ready with my next. Although I tried hard to make him understand that I had a family to consider, a demanding job, was often away on business and that my mother took up much of my free time, he complained that he heard from me all too rarely.

The more I got to know Pee-Wee, the more I found myself wondering who he really was, what he had done and whether one day I would be able to visit him; and, not least, what the outcome would be.

With every letter he wrote, he opened up more and more, and after a while he also began to tell me something about his childhood.

CHILDHOOD

What I'm fixing to tell you please don't say anything to my mother about this because we have had words over this. I was 3 years old when I got burned (1968). My sister set me on fire and lock me out of the house early in the morning hours. So this day I remember clear just as it happen yesterday. Anyway my parents told me that I set myself on fire playing with matches. I can understand why they told me that because they didn't want me to hate my sister and I don't. The lady next door had come home from work and found me in the yard on fire. […] She got hold of my parents and they took me to the hospital. […] No one thought I would live. But I did. My right arm was burned so bad the doctors said I'd never be able to use it again. Well, they didn't know me because I have full use of my arm and have had surgery on it and it is better than before.

As an adult, he said, he had a normal relationship with his sister Jane, although they had never agreed on what really happened on that fateful day in 1968. No one believed that he would live, but he did, which helped me to understand the special treatment accorded him at home. He was the centre of attention, the family favourite.

He was introduced to marihuana at the tender age of nine. This notwithstanding, he described his childhood as a happy one. Highly talented, by the time he was eleven he was not only playing the cornet in a band and boxing, he was also playing baseball and both European and American football.

Looking back, what he regretted most was what had happened to him when he was thirteen. That was when he met his nemesis in the shape of his two-year-older second cousin, who was already a confirmed drug addict. It was this fifteen-year-old, himself still little more than a child, who so disastrously got him hooked.

Let me tell you how I started using hard drugs. My cousin who introduced me to marihuana came to our house and asked if I wanted to help him to roof a barn. I said sure. We left and went to his friend's house and they all were putting dope (crank) in a spoon and drawing it up in a syringe and putting it in the vein in their arms. My cousin told me, once I had done this I would never want any other drug and this was the best way to do it, so I let him put drugs in my arm. From that day on I was addicted to drugs. I look back on the day at the age of 13 when my innocence was stolen from me.

I didn't know that that day would be the one I'd remember the most, not only was my innocence taken from me but so were

my dreams. I had dreams that never came
true. I caused my family a lot of pain, but they
never realized WHY I was on the path I was
on. My innocence was stolen at the age of 13.

Enclosed with the letter was this poem:

Little Boy Lost
The memories still haunt me,
even after all these years.
You still make me cry
You stole my innocence
You took my trust
And now it is turned to dust
The beginning of a battle
That many will fight me for
And will never win
It was alright, you always said
And I believed in you
But children always believe in fantasies.
I need to understand 'Why'
But I could never talk to you
Just exactly what you did to me.
The pain lives in my heart
my mind and memories
If I could only just forget
and relieve it every time I think of drugs
This is the pain I need to escape from
I hope one day that I can find the key
And then one day I can escape to have the freedom

Let me tell you a little about myself:
The essence and quality of the life I lived from
the age of 13 to 17 wasn't that of a saint and I
had to endure many hardships, overcoming
obstacles that seemed impossible and endless.
Drugs and alcohol took their toll on me,
depriving me of an innocent childhood that
was set in motion on January 10, 1965 [his
birth date] by two people that I dearly love.
They showed me that love and joy that
parents should show to their children, but
around the corner, waiting for me, wasn't the
innocence of a child, but that of a beast
waiting to take control of another helpless
child, poisoning its mind.

He often wrote about his parents. He was proud of
them and retained many happy memories of his home
life. He also spoke fondly of his brother and two
sisters. To me, his parents seemed to have been
unnecessarily strict, and I found it hard to accept that
when he was a child they had regularly beaten him.
On the other hand, I realized that they must have felt
increasingly powerless in the face of his many petty
crimes. Pee-Wee admitted that he had several times
served prison sentences for burglary and larceny.

My family wasn't rich, but they gave us their divine love, taught us right from wrong. Me and my siblings didn't always have the best things in life, my parents worked hard to provide us. I was what is called 'the black sheep of the family'. Better known as a rebellious kid. Back in those days when disciplined for getting in trouble, the extension cord and fishing pole were used for spanking, which I got often. I thought I knew it all at the age of 14. I ran away from home, used drugs and had my first encounter with the police.

I remember it as though it was yesterday. It was a turning point in my life, because after that day I never had another whipping from my parents. I guess they realized that I was getting too old for that kind of punishment.

This traumatic experience, and the scars left by his burns, had remained with him all his life. He often spoke about the fire and what it had done to him. It was clearly etched deep in his memory.

At times I wish I was never born, I'd go to the lake to swim and had to wear a shirt and people would always ask, why do you wear a shirt? So, I just had those thoughts in my head: Why do people care about my outer appearance? My scars? I've thought of suicide before, but that does not solve any problems at all.

Like other children I had a heart and that is where true Beauty lies.

When he was fifteen he set off on what he described as a fishing trip with a difference:

> It was in the summer of 1980, I was sitting alone on the bank of the Red River, no one around but the sounds of birds and insects speaking to each other in their own language with no worries in the world that was created for them. I sat and put some bait on a hook and cast my fishing rod to a spot that I knew would lure a big fish to my tasty bait. I put my fishing rod down and then took out a gram of white powder, known as speed. I reached in and pulled a spoon and syringe from my back pack. As I dumped a ¼ gram in the spoon I added 15 units of water to break down the powder. I mixed it real good and then drew the contents up in the syringe and pumped the air bubbles out, pushing the air out of the syringe, careful not to waste the high that was to come. I tied my arm off, opening and closing my hand in order to make my veins show. I then eased the syringe into my vein, careful not to go all the way through. With the syringe in I slowly pushed the drug into the vein, feeling the tingle caused by the drug's taking effect. I sat tasting the drug that just went into my veins.
>
> When I came back to earth I realized I was all alone. I realized that I had been sitting in the same spot for three hours and it was time for me to head home. Walking through the woods, everything seemed very quiet. I could no longer hear the birds singing, it was like they knew what I had done was wrong.

I reflect back to this day in my life and little
did I know I could have changed destiny with
a few simple words, 'This is wrong', but as
Fate would have it, I went down a long and
painful road that seemed to go on for ever and
ever. My dreams were eliminated by poison.
At the age of 17 I had been released from a
juvenile home for troubled youths that had
problems living at home. I spent almost a year
there. Back at home life was still tough. I had
dropped out of school and started going to
clubs, using more drugs and staying out late at
night. So my family moved to Oklahoma to
get me away from my friends. But that was not
the problem. I knew how to get drugs and
could spot a drug user in any crowd. It wasn't
long before I was back in with the same type of
people as before.

In a letter he wrote to me some six months after we
first became acquainted, he recounted one of the
many dramatic episodes that marked his young life. It
revolved around his best friend, Jamie. This is how he
described it:

> Marit, I was 17 years old and watched my best
> friend take a gun and blow his brains out. We
> were doing drugs one day, about 6 of us, and
> Jamie said 'I wonder what it's like to die,' and
> he pulled out a gun, put it to his head and
> pulled the trigger. I seen his brains splatter all
> over the walls. Me, Jamie, my brother and his
> brother went to boy scouts together. Every
> time you seen me he was with me.

I haven't talked to anyone about this in 10
years. That's been a long time, but back then I
didn't want to talk about what I saw because
Jamie was like my brother.

As he wrote, one would think that such a horrific
experience would put a person off drugs for ever.
Sadly, in his case it didn't:

I should have learned from what happen to
my friend but it seemed that I needed more
drugs to deal with all the pains I had in my
heart. Now you know a little more about my
life, maybe you know why I'm as strong as I
am now. It's not easy to be strong,
determination, willpower and love have made
me the person I am.

SENTENCED TO DEATH

After having corresponded with him for some eighteen months or more, I finally received an answer to the question I had never dared to ask: Why was he on Death Row?

Before the family moved to Oklahoma, they had lived in Denison, a town in Texas. As a youngster, Pee-Wee had often helped a neighbour, Lula Mae Denning. Whenever she was in need of assistance, she would come over to enlist his aid, and for a long time he helped her, often up to three times a week. For years he regularly mowed her lawn; in return, she would give him a small sum of money.

> I have nothing to hide from you at all at why I'm here. I was accused of killing a woman that I had known all my life. I was accused of going in her house, robbing her and beating her to death. There was four people in all arrested for this crime. One received the life sentence and the other two were released.

Without any prompting on my part, Pee-Wee asked his mother to send me the documents relating to his trial, to give me a better understanding of why he was where he was. His sister Jane had been a witness at the trial and his mother had been present throughout, avidly following all that transpired. She was there, too, when her son was sentenced to the law's ultimate penalty; on that dread occasion she was the only member of the family present.

> When you get the documents from the Court, you can ask all the questions you want. I will be very honest with you and you must also know that I am trusting you with things that my lawyer has told me not to share with anyone.
>
> My own mother has never read any of the legal documents that I am sending to you. I know that I do need help in getting off death row and I have hard facts that prove I am innocent and I need to talk to you face to face and have you get all my trial records, because you can do more out there than I can from in here.

A few days later I received a bulky envelope from Pee-Wee's mother Stella, who was still living in Oklahoma. The envelope contained a jumble of yellowing newspaper cuttings and court records. Also enclosed was a brief note from Pee-Wee's mother. It was written on a small card with a floral design in almost illegible handwriting; the spelling too left a lot to be desired and I had great difficulty in deciphering it.

One thing I did manage to grasp, however, and that was this: 'People like you are good to have – for people like me'. What impressed me most, though, was that she had entrusted me with all she possessed in the way of original official documents relating to her son's case and sentence, all with detailed accounts of his previous convictions and other offences that were still under investigation. Many of these were copies of the legal proceedings leading up to the death sentence and the judge's summing-up.

One of the newspaper cuttings carried a photograph of the dead woman. It showed a good-looking, smiling, elderly lady with a long pearl necklace[1] draped twice around her neck.

Stella had also taken the trouble to make and enclose an audio tape recording. She spoke in a pronounced Oklahoma dialect I found hard to understand, but she had a rich vocabulary -- which explained why she preferred to talk rather than write.

It took me a long time to understand the legal jargon in which the official documents were phrased, but perusal of the newspaper cuttings enabled me to follow the course of the two-week-long trial from day to day. I discovered that it had been the only murder trial held in the 336th Grayson County Court for many years. The prosecution had prepared the ground well, taking no less than five weeks just to select the twelve members of the jury from a pool of 112.[2] The judge was Ray Grisham, the district attorney Bob Jarvis. I discovered that on a number of occasions in the past the latter had been involved in proceedings relating to Pee-Wee's earlier offences.

The trial opened on 14 October 1990 and came to an end on the 27th of the same month. The local press gave extensive coverage to the trial, which was held in open court. The defence did all they could to sow doubt as to Pee-Wee's guilt and made much of the fact that the court should take into account that there had been a great deal of public pre-judgment of the accused and that much had been made of Pee-Wee's previous convictions.[3]

Before Pee-Wee and his three companions were arrested and charged with murder, a close relative of the deceased had been apprehended by the police. From the newspaper cuttings[4] I learned that, the morning the body was discovered, the man in question had been involved in a dispute with the victim, but that he had subsequently been released and absolved from blame. Then, ten days after the murder, the police received an anonymous telephone call claiming that Pee-Wee was the person responsible; he was arrested the same day. While in custody, he signed a declaration to the effect that he knew he had the right to remain silent but that he voluntarily waived this right. In his first written voluntary statement he claimed, among other things, that he had never been anywhere near the scene of the crime while in Denison and that he had no idea of who the perpetrators were.

Despite this, in a second statement, also voluntary, he admitted to having been in the house together with another man (whom he did not name).

He said that the two had gone there with the intention of stealing money with which to buy drugs, and that Lula Mae Denning had let them in. He further said that the plan was for him to keep her occupied while his accomplice rifled her handbag. He went on to say that he had been treated to a bowl of ice cream and then been asked to go out for a newspaper; when he returned, it was to find his friend arguing with Lula Mae and belabouring her with a baseball bat. At that point he had fled.

Pee-Wee later retracted his second statement and reiterated his claim of never having been there at all; he said the same thing in several of his letters to me. He described his statement about having been in the house as being 'miles from the truth' and claimed that it had been made under duress. He maintained that he had been high on drugs and alcohol and would never have signed anything like that in normal circumstances:

> 99 per cent of the bad things I have done I was never caught for, but the only thing I never did I got the death sentence for. I admit that I had a drug problem, I am not an angel, but I am NOT a murderer, even if the State tried to make me one. The weapon did not have my fingerprints on it and there is a lot of evidence against another person.

The police claimed that Pee-Wee had a wedding ring on his finger when he was arrested and that it had belonged to the dead woman; the prosecution made much of this in court. Pee-Wee, for his part, maintained that he had bought the ring on a date prior to the murder and had it valued by a goldsmith, who had said that it was seven years old.

The newspaper cuttings Stella had sent me proved a rich source of information, some of which was by no means to Pee-Wee's advantage. For example, his fingerprints were said to have been found on the bowl in which Lula Mae Denning had served him ice cream shortly before being battered to death. Not surprisingly, the press made much of this too – of how an innocent woman had been brutally murdered after having shown her visitor such generosity.[5] Was this a bowl that hadn't been properly washed? There is no means of knowing, but that was what Pee-Wee now argued. He said that for many years he had been accustomed to dropping in at the murdered woman's house but – and it was a big 'but' – he had also said, both in a statement and in the course of an interrogation, that he hadn't seen her since he was seventeen. According to the newspaper reports, forensic evidence pointed solely at Pee-Wee, though none of his fingerprints were found on what was assumed to be the murder weapon, the baseball bat.

Was Pee-Wee telling the truth? I was utterly confused and didn't know what to think.

Pee-Wee was the only one of the four men originally charged to be condemned to death. His presumed accomplices were given life sentences.[6]

In Pee-Wee's case the decisive factor was a statement made in court by another prisoner, who claimed that Pee-Wee had told him that he had beaten Lula Mae Denning to death:

> The reason I am here in the first place is that one person in court said that I told him I confessed to the crime, which is A LIE!!

Among the documents I had received from Stella was a sheet of paper in Pee-Wee's handwriting; addressed to his then attorney, it was an ardent refutation of this witness's testimony:

> Mr. A. Wright also knows that I never spoke to the witness because I didn´t like him. R. Smith could have told you the same. The two of them could have confirmed that I never discuss my case with anyone. The only thing I ever told, was that I had nothing to do with what I was convicted for.

 Pee-Wee had appended the addresses of both Wright and Smith, who had been in prison with him, and urged his attorney to contact them.

According to Pee-Wee, the witness concerned had testified against him in the hope that his sentence would be reduced as a result. In the event, the man was released from prison the day after signing a statement in which he swore that his fellow prisoner had admitted murdering Lula Mae Denning.[7] Pee-Wee was himself never allowed to say anything in court, despite his wish to do so. The decision not to allow him to testify was taken by the defence attorney. This seems to be standard practice, to prevent a defendant incriminating himself.

Whatever the truth of the matter, there is no doubt that from that point on, and also while on Death Row, Pee-Wee fought desperately to prove his innocence. In his letters he complained at length about how he had been wrongfully convicted. As he saw it, there were only two alternatives: acquittal or a death sentence. Prisoners under sentence of death do sometimes have their sentences commuted to life or something less severe if they confess, but there was never any question of this in Pee-Wee's case. He insisted that he would never confess to something he had not done.[8] From the day he was locked in his cell on Death Row, his greatest wish was to be granted a live hearing.[9] This would enable him, in conjunction with his attorney, to present his case anew to the judge who had sentenced him; it would also enable him to call new witnesses. Pee-Wee was convinced that such a hearing would afford him an opportunity to present new evidence and thereby to persuade the judge either to pronounce him Not Guilty or reopen the case.

> I can write page after page showing how the state fabricated this case on me and the people that lied on me, there is endless amounts of it. That's why it is best to have the trial record, that way you read everything as was said in my trial. Anyway, I will write more on this and fill you in on what my co-defendant wrote in

his statement. You know it is very frustrating to have to be on death row for a crime that I had nothing to do with and it's hard to find people that is willing to get involved with power.

You ask me if there was some church that I could get to help me, sure there is a bunch of them that believe in the death penalty and they wouldn't mind helping the state put a needle in my arm and fill it up with poison.

I just received some documents from the FBI concerning the beating I received from the police the day I was arrested. I will send them to you and let you view them. The case was dismissed because they felt the beating wasn't that serious. It really doesn't matter if the beating was serious or not, the fact is the police beat me while I was in handcuffs.

Pee-Wee wrote to me that he did not trust anyone in authority, not even the prison chaplain. He consistently refused to enter into detail about his case, as he was afraid that some of the prison staff might get hold of his letters and prevent me doing what he had in mind. He wrote that when I visited him in the States, he would let me have all the names and addresses of the men who were involved in the crime. He wanted me to get in touch with them and record all our conversations, so that they would subsequently be unable to change their stories in court. He was also of the opinion that all names should be changed, to make sure that I could not be sued if ever I wrote a book about his case.

I was very dispirited on reading this letter, the thirteenth I had received from him. Quite simply, I thought he was asking too much of me. How could he expect me to contact a lot of people who were totally unknown to me and who might have played a part in the murder? I didn't even know whether he was telling me the truth. I also began to wonder just what his expectations were: did he really believe that I could get him acquitted?

In response, I told him that I had written to a number of relevant organizations and public authorities in the United States to request their help. I concluded by saying that I could do no more.

This notwithstanding, he was still very keen for me to write a book about him – which could have been one of the reasons he was so frank with me.

Very early on in our relationship, I realized that he was far from impressed with the lawyers he had been allocated. This came as no surprise. Not a few people within the American judiciary have drawn attention to the fact that public-appointed defence lawyers are overworked, underpaid and all too often lacking in experience as well, with the result that the outcome of many a trial and law suit is swayed by these selfsame factors.[10] There is little doubt that, by and large, it is the poor who suffer most grievously under the American judicial system. Pee-Wee had personally written to a number of private law firms in an endeavour to persuade them to take up his case

50

with the judge who had sentenced him originally, but
to no avail. He was, after all, to all intents and
purposes penniless:

> I have been writing to law firms trying to get
> them involved in my case, but all my attempts
> so far have failed, but every stamp I get I use it
> for that purpose, except the ones I put away
> for writing to you. I am no quitter, even
> though at times I do think all my efforts are
> useless, but no matter what my thoughts are I
> keep going. I feel that you could share more
> with me than you do, more of yourself that is.
> One thing you will never have to worry about
> and that is me stop writing you. I would
> NEVER stop writing you and there isn't
> anything in this world that could make me.
> I don't only need help to get off death row, but
> I also need help to pass the time I have on my
> hands, especially when I am lonely. You know
> they say that worrying is a disease and it's bad
> for you to worry. I look at life and accept what
> it gives me each day and I have to take the
> good with the bad. I have you in my life, and it
> keeps me going.

> My cousin witnessed against me during the
> trial. He helped the state to give me the death
> penalty. I don´t pity him at all but I do not
> hate him either. He is still on drugs. He knows
> what he did to me, but he doesn´t care. All his
> brothers are drug dealers and have been to
> prison for it. Wait till I can show you what the
> State did to me. I am sure you will be furious,
> but I need a

powerful person to force them to let me go. If I
could have hired a good lawyer from the start,
I would not have been here.

My younger brother was sent to prison last
month for drug dealing. I know he should
have learned from my mistakes but he didn´t.
My mother was very upset and I became very,
very angry with him.

In Pee-Wee's view, the illegal trade in narcotics was
the scourge of present-day America. It was
dependency on drugs that had led him into crime, and
now he was afraid that his young brother was on the
same downward path. He was outraged by the
authorities' failure to do more to combat the racket.
He said that, although many individuals and
organizations were devoting themselves to the
problem, people high up in Congress and the Senate
preferred to close their eyes to what was happening. I
could tell from the way he wrote how deeply he felt
about this issue:

This isn't the land of the free, this is the land
of corruption, greed and lies. I would give
everything I have to leave this country, I hate
the Government, it stinks and they are fascists.
[. . .] Everything in this world is only
temporary anyway. I don't know what is in
there for me in the future, so I lives the day
being happy and peaceful.
I have been writing on this letter for
three hours now and it doesn't seem like it.

I was beginning to realize that in the light of the policy then current in Texas, Pee-Wee had landed in the worst state in the union when it came to ending one's days on Death Row.

In the year that I first came to know him, 1993, of the thirty-eight people executed in the USA, no fewer than seventeen of them were put to death in Texas. That was 45 per cent of the total.[11]

OKLAHOMA

As far as I could make out, Pee-Wee had little to do
with his fellow prisoners. It was clear to me that what
he wished for – and was most in need of – was visitors
from the world outside. The two of us had now been
corresponding for fourteen months, and I had begun
to feel an increasing desire to see him in the flesh.

I had long been toying with the idea of visiting
my son and his new Spanish partner in Atlanta,
Georgia, and I also very much wanted to see again my
sole grandchild, who had just turned three.

The thought occurred to me that I might be
able to combine my trip to Atlanta with a visit to Pee-
Wee. To this end I phoned the famous or, more
correctly, infamous Ellis Unit 1 at the State
Penitentiary in Huntsville to ask how to go about
obtaining permission to visit him. Pee-Wee had told
me earlier that it would take about three weeks to get
permission, so I assumed that, as there were still six
weeks left before I was due to leave Norway, I would
have no difficulty in getting to see him.

When I rang, I was put through to the
Warden's Office, where I was told that, as a
preliminary, I had to inform the prisoner concerned
that I wished to visit him. A check would then have to
be undertaken to ascertain when he had last altered

his visitors list, as changes to it could only be made at six-month intervals.

The young woman who took my call kept me waiting for a couple of minutes and on her return informed me that Pee-Wee, whom she referred to as Murphy, had recently changed his list and that my name wasn't among the ten names on it. That meant that I would not be able to visit him until March the following year at the earliest – always assuming that he wanted me to.

March lay six months ahead. I asked if they made exceptions for visitors from abroad, only to be told that they didn't. What about journalists? I asked. No, was the answer, I would still be classed as an ordinary visitor. I then asked if I would be allowed into his cell once I got to see him, only to be told that that was out of the question and that we would have to converse through a thick plate of glass and that there could be no physical contact. Disappointed though I was, I couldn't help feeling a slight sense of relief.

I then asked how often we would be allowed to see one another once permission was granted, and was informed that prisoners were permitted one visit a month. However, it transpired that if I were granted special permission, which I would be, having come from so far away, I would be able to meet him twice, on two consecutive days, for four hours each day. Visits were permitted on weekdays only, never on Saturdays or Sundays.

Armed with this information, I wrote to Pee-Wee and asked him to put me on his visitors list, just in case, though without disclosing that I was planning to come and see him.

Ten days later I received a letter telling me that his mother had been to visit him. He was very happy about it, as it had been a long time since he had last seen her.

That decided me, and I resolved to try inviting myself to visit his family.

***

Few of my friends could understand why I wanted to go to Oklahoma at the end of November 1994. The one exception was my husband, who urged me to follow my heart and do just that. His positive attitude apart, there was no shortage of warnings about visiting Pee-Wee's closest relatives, people I knew nothing at all about. One of my friends insisted that I was unbelievably naïve, while my mother was beside herself with worry. After all, all I knew about Pee-Wee's family was what he himself had told me – and he was a man under sentence of death!

I couldn't help wondering whether his parents would show me the woods he had roamed as a boy and the streams and rivers where he had spent so many hours fishing. On the tape his mother had sent me, she said that he always came home with a catch. She also told me about the band he had played in and how he had played soccer and American football with his friends, as well as how intelligent he was and how well he had done at school.

My parents will be more than happy to see you, and you can stay with them as long as you want. You will have a very comfortable bed to sleep in and access to a private bathroom. You will be treated like family when you stay with them. I have sent a special request to the Warden if he can grant you a visit here as well.

Some weeks later I found myself gazing down at Dallas, the city where, thirty years earlier, President John F. Kennedy had been so cold-bloodedly assassinated. I had plenty of time for contemplation as, owing to the heavy traffic, we were compelled to circle the airport for half an hour before we were able to land. I also found myself wondering what might lie ahead.

Shortly afterwards I emerged into the Arrivals Hall of the city's enormous Fort Worth international airport and eagerly scanned the assembled crowd. I sincerely hoped that Pee-Wee's mother had received my last letter and that she and his sister Jane would be there to meet me.

I needn't have worried. There they were, right up in the front row, waving madly, their faces all smiles. I could see at a glance how, with their characteristic Native-American features, alike Pee-Wee and his mother were.

We all hugged each other warmly.

Although very much overweight, Stella, Pee-Wee's mother, was still a handsome woman. She had thick, near-white hair gathered high on her head and cascading down her back. Her strong, black eyebrows bore witness to the fact that her hair had once been equally dark. On her stockingless feet she was wearing sandals. When I asked her how she could go about more or less barefooted late in November, she laughed and said she was accustomed to going without shoes all year round. I also commented on her beautiful hair. 'It's white because of Pee-Wee,' she said, laughing through her throaty smoker's cough. 'Every one of those white hairs I owe to him. All my other children have made out all right, though some of them have caused me plenty of worries over the years.'

Stella not only had problems in breathing, she also had difficulty in holding herself upright.

Tall and slim, with her shoulder-length hair and spectacles, unlike her mother, Pee-Wee's sister Jane looked like any other young American girl. I couldn't help feeling relieved at how welcoming and friendly the two of them were. They told me it had taken them three hours to get to the airport.

Now I was about to accompany them on the return journey to the small town of Hugo, close to where Oklahoma bordered on Texas. This was America's heartland, and it was here I was going to stay for three days with Pee-Wee's family.

Although we had only just met, I felt that I already knew them, to some extent anyway, as Pee-Wee had given me vivid descriptions of them all.

Stella was forty-eight, his father some years older. There were four grown-up children in the family, though none of them were now living at home. There were several grandchildren, too; I hoped I would meet some of them as well.

I eased myself into the back seat of Jane's small car and made myself comfortable amid a litter of empty Coca-Cola bottles and crumpled newspapers. It was already eight o'clock in the evening and Hugo was nearly 750 miles distant. Stella eased her bulk in beside her daughter, who was driving; I couldn't help noticing that neither of them fastened their seat belt. What they did do, however, was to light a cigarette. They offered me one but I declined, though not without a pang of regret that I no longer smoked.

Jane drove fast, but fortunately she was as steady as a rock. I couldn't help reflecting that she was Pee-Wee's two-year-older sister and that she had been with him in that dramatic fire -- and also that she had had her first child at the tender age of thirteen, a child that had died shortly after birth. She had subsequently had three boys by another man.

Before long we were out on the highway and Jane and her mother began to talk about Pee-Wee. The prison in which he was held was four hours by bus *south* of Dallas airport, whereas to reach his home we were travelling *north*. Stella was greatly distressed by the fact that my application to visit him had been turned down.

'Next time I'm in Texas, I'll make sure to go and see him,' I promised her.

I was already used to the way Stella spoke, thanks to
the tapes she had sent me. She radiated warmth and
good humour, and after a while I began to understand
more of what she said. Her husky laugh was never far
away, but I could sense the sadness behind it.

'When he was a kid, his father and I often
went fishing with him,' she said.

I already knew that, as Pee-Wee had several
times told me about it in his letters. In one of them he
wrote that he had once borrowed a boat and spent an
enjoyable day fishing from that.

The conversation flowed easily as we bowled along in
Jane's beat-up old car, notwithstanding the fact that
the family had recently discovered from a news flash
on a local television channel that a date had been set
for Pee-Wee's execution. It was scheduled for
February, which was only a little more than two
months away. Pee-Wee himself had never said a word
about it, neither to his family nor to me. He had no
idea of how closely the members of his family were
able to follow his case through the media. I was
surprised that they could talk about it so matter-of-
factly. The reason was probably that neither Stella nor
Jane believed that the sentence would actually be
carried out. In the United States, prisoners under
sentence of death are afforded ample opportunities to
appeal, which explains why so many of them languish
for years on Death Row. At that time Pee-Wee had
only submitted a few appeals, all of which had been
rejected.

'He rang us yesterday, as it happens,' Stella said. 'That's because he knew you were coming. It was the first phone call we'd had from him for three years.'

Prisoners are allowed one telephone call to their family every three months. Pee-Wee had told me that he had little contact with his relatives, but maintained that they meant a lot to him even so. The only member of the family to visit him occasionally was his mother. His father, on the other hand, had never been near the prison; Stella thought it was because he simply couldn't face it. Pee-Wee's younger brother and two sisters hadn't been there either.

'I always feel physically sick when I've been to see him and I've often had to go into hospital afterwards,' Stella said, a catch in her voice. She paused briefly before continuing: 'I've had three heart attacks since Pee-Wee received the death sentence, and my husband has had one.'

'When someone's sentenced to death,' Jane added, 'the whole family is sentenced with him.' Stella nodded in agreement.

Both mother and daughter were at a loss to understand how the American state could spend money on teaching Pee-Wee criminology and economics while at the same time aiming to put him to death. 'They'd have done better to find him a good lawyer,' said Jane vehemently.

Both Jane and her mother adamantly refused to believe that Pee-Wee had done what he had been sentenced for.

'He even underwent a private lie-detector test that proved that he didn't kill her,' Stella said, lighting yet another cigarette, 'though it couldn't confirm that he hadn't been there when she was killed.'

Jane lit another cigarette too.

Pee-Wee had told me about this test in one of his letters, and I had read in a newspaper report Stella had sent me that the court had refused to take the test results into account. Stella acknowledged that the case was complex in the extreme, but insisted that Pee-Wee could prove his innocence and that it ought to be reopened. Pee-Wee was resolved to work to this end until the last.

I still didn't know what to think. I had had great difficulty in understanding some of the documents Stella had sent me. I had brought them back for her in my hand luggage, many of them, I'm ashamed to say, unread for this very reason.

The stars were twinkling in the night sky as we crossed the state line into Oklahoma and neared Hugo in Choctaw County. Like Pee-Wee and his family, most of the local inhabitants had Native-American blood in their veins. This was because, towards the close of the nineteenth century, America's Indian population, mainly from the east coast regions, had been forcibly transplanted to Oklahoma. The results were disastrous. In this small town – it had a population of little more than seven thousand – there were on average seven murders a year!

Pee-Wee's parents' house was an unpretentious but
homely dwelling in a poor part of the town. His father
came out to greet us and took in my suitcase and bags.
We were also greeted by two cute little Pekinese dogs,
Tippy and April. April was a born guard dog. She
stationed herself beside Ivan senior and growled
menacingly whenever someone came too near. In
contrast to his wife, Ivan was slightly built and quick
on his feet. He was a quarter Choctaw Indian and
three quarters Irish, hence the family surname,
Murphy.

I was given a room of my own, a newly
refurbished little bedroom. There were colourful
Indian hangings on the walls and stuffed animals on a
chest-of-drawers, among them a fox which seemed to
follow my every movement with its unblinking glass
eyes. Pee-Wee had sent home a number of works of
art he had made with the simple tools available to him
in the prison, many of them painstakingly crafted from
toothpicks. The whole room -- it had been his
bedroom when he was growing up – was full of things
he had made with his own hands.

The narrow passage leading to the living room
and kitchen was lined with family photographs. My
attention was caught by a large, framed picture of a
sweet little girl, her chin cupped in her hand, sitting in
a chair that was far too big for her small body. I put
her age at about five or six. She was wearing a white,
lace-trimmed floral dress and her bare legs with their

white socks were tucked into red strap shoes. She was smiling broadly for the benefit of the photographer. I asked Stella who she was.

'That's Pee-Wee's daughter,' she replied, 'I think so, anyway. She looks like him, that's for sure.'

She went on to confess that she had never been able to relate to the child, apart from having received the picture and hanging it up.

'I understand that her mother's on drugs. I've no idea what's become of her, but I'm pretty sure she's my granddaughter. Pee-Wee knows nothing about her either, other than that he's her father. I've more than enough problems as it is, so maybe it's best she knows nothing about us,' Stella said with a sigh.

I couldn't hide my astonishment at this unexpected revelation. Why hadn't Pee-Wee told me that he had a daughter when I myself had told him all about my own family in letter after letter and he knew so much about all my relatives? It began to dawn on me that there were things about him that he had been keeping back.

Stella then asked me if I'd like something to eat, but I said no. Overcome by jet lag and fatigue, I decided that the time had come to call it a day. Despite my tiredness, it took me a long time to fall asleep, not least because of the insistent noise of the television in the living room next door, added to which was the ever-present clucking of hens, the caterwauling of countless cats, the barking of dogs and the screeching of tyres from the cars racing through the narrow streets.

I was awakened next morning by the crowing of a cockerel close by, and in the course of the day that followed I got to meet several of the family's neighbours, who dropped in to say hello. I was also introduced to Stella's mother, Helen, who had been in bed when I arrived the day before. She had been a friend of the woman Pee-Wee was accused of having killed and actually lived in Denison, over the border in Texas. This was just a brief visit -- probably to check out the family's guest from Norway. Over a lavish breakfast of bacon and eggs Helen told me about the morning when she went to pick up her friend Lula Mae, only to find the house ringed by police cars and

cordoned off with yellow tape. Sometime later she
heard that Pee-Wee had been arrested and charged
with her friend's murder. She shook her head sadly
and said that she simply couldn't understand it.

'It was terrible,' she said. 'I'd talked to her only
the previous evening.'

I later got to meet the Murphys' youngest
daughter, Grace, who came over with her young son.
I was also introduced to Stella's best friend, a woman
who had once been a snake handler and who had
remained steadfastly at Stella's side in the courtroom
throughout Pee-Wee's trial. I felt that I was being
thoroughly vetted and that they all had hopes that I
would be able to do something to help Pee-Wee. I
have no means of knowing if I was right, as no one as
much as hinted at such a thing and everyone was as
pleasant and friendly as could be. My stay was one
long round of coffee drinking, over-eating and talking
for hours on end. As seems to be common in America,
the television was on all the time, though no one
appeared to be watching it; the only exception was
when there was a rodeo on. Then everyone perked up,
lit cigarettes and crowded round the set. I discovered
that Pee-Wee's oldest nephew – he was sixteen – was
training to be a professional rodeo rider; not
surprisingly, they were all immensely proud of him.

Jane and I pored over old photo albums full of
pictures of Pee-Wee: photographs of when he was
small, class photos, scenes of Pee-Wee playing a
variety of musical instruments and even shots of him

mowing lawns – including one of him together with
the old lady whom he was accused of having
murdered.

Stella had once been a nursing auxiliary at the
city's one and only nursing home, but had had to give
it up because of poor health. Now she spent her days
making Indian trinkets, pretty earrings in all the
colours of the rainbow, from small plastic beads. It
transpired that she never sold them but just gave them
away. She told me that she only made them to give
her something meaningful to do. She later gave me a
pair for myself.

In one old album I came across a photograph
of a handsome-looking man in Air Force uniform;
taken in Yokohama, Japan, during the Vietnam war,
it was of Stella's husband Ivan, Pee-Wee's father.

Following his discharge, Ivan had been
employed by the municipal Highways Department,
but when his son was sentenced to death he had lost
his job; fortunately, however, reason prevailed and he
was reinstated two years later.

***

I sat upright in what had once been Pee-Wee's bed
and went over in my mind all that I knew about him.
It was just over a year since we had begun to write to
one another and now here I was in his childhood
home in what was, for me, an American state I knew

next to nothing about, together with his parents and
the rest of his family. It was a surrealistic situation
altogether.

The household noises seemed to grow ever
louder.

Stella was busy in the kitchen, baking a cake,
with a stew simmering on the gas stove. Her mother
was perched on the sofa, legs tucked away beneath
her. I was surprised at how supple and agile she was
for a woman of sixty-five who had given birth to nine
children. Two of her children were in prison for minor
offences and Pee-Wee, her grandson, was languishing
on Death Row. Small wonder, then, that her eyes
were so full of sorrow and despair. Totally lacking in
Stella's buoyant good humour, she kept her feelings
very much to herself and rarely spoke more than a few
words at a time.

Stella and her husband couldn't do enough for
me. I assumed that Pee-Wee had told them we were
planning to write a book about him. That was all
right, but what worried me was that they might be
thinking that I could bring his plight to the notice of
an international public. Although no one ever said as
much, I had the feeling that the family's unarticulated
expectations regarding what I could do for their errant
son and brother, cast a dark shadow over what was, in
all other respects, a very pleasant stay. I couldn't help
wondering, though, why they thought I, of all people,
would be able to do something for him when nobody
else could. For my part, I couldn't see what else

I *could* do other than to continue to write to him and perhaps visit him one day.

I asked Stella what she was baking.

'I promised Pee-Wee I'd bake you a Mississippi Mud Pie,' she said in reply. 'It's his favourite cake, you see. He's not had any himself for six years, though.'

The finished product proved to be a little too sweet for my taste when we had it for dessert, but I was intrigued by what went into its making: butter, sugar, multiple eggs, chocolate, cocoa, pecan nuts and finely chopped marshmallows. It was topped with butter, icing sugar, cocoa, melted chocolate and thick cream and was undoubtedly the most satisfying and substantial cake I had ever eaten!

One evening Stella and Ivan invited me to join them at the monthly dance held at the nursing home where Stella had once worked as an auxiliary nurse. I was told that in happier days, when he was small, Pee-Wee had often entertained the residents with music and songs. I piled into their old pick-up, wedged between Stella and her husband, for the short drive to the nursing home.

On arrival we were welcomed with open arms by a throng of patients and staff and warmly embraced by all and sundry. I found that many of the residents were mentally ill, but when a scratch orchestra struck up for dancing, it wasn't long before the floor was crowded with eager participants, some of them in wheelchairs.

I fell into conversation with the organizer, who was well acquainted with Stella and Ivan.

'The two of them do a great job by coming to our dances,' she said. 'It can be tough going and they don't *have* to do it. When you consider all they've been through because of Pee-Wee, I think it's really very good of them. The patients think the world of them.'

Stella's craving for a smoke frequently drew her out onto the terrace, and on one occasion I went out with her. Alone together in the fading light of a cool November evening, with the incessant sound of katydids as a background, Stella again began to talk about Pee-Wee.

'Everyone around here knows about him,' she said sadly, 'so here we can be ourselves.'

At that moment her husband came out to join us, he too prompted by the urge for a smoke.

'We had to move several times,' he told me. 'First we lived in Denison in Texas, then we moved to Oklahoma City in the hope that things would be better there. They weren't, they were worse. Drugs were everywhere. After that we came here to this little town. There are drug dealers here, too, on every street corner, so it's no good keeping on moving. We just have to try to make the best of it. Everyone knows us and knows the burden we are forced to bear. That's why the bad guys leave us alone.'

Stella and Ivan hadn't only Pee-Wee to worry about. As Pee-Wee had already told me, his younger brother was in prison for drug dealing. As it had been his first offence, however, he had been leniently dealt

with and sentenced to only a few months behind bars,
which meant that he was due to be released in a few
weeks' time. 'If only Pee-Wee could get someone to reopen his case,' Ivan said wistfully. 'We can't afford to
pay for the help he needs ourselves.'

To round off the evening I was invited home
to Peggy and Bob, two family friends. There were ten
of us in all, seated round a kitchen table covered with
an oilcloth. I was served with ice tea – the others all
took coffee -- while Peggy busied herself cutting a
chocolate cake into squares before handing a piece to
each of us. No alcohol was served, neither there nor at
Stella and Ivan's.

The following day I went for a short walk by
myself to have a look at the neighbourhood. I
ventured only a few hundred yards from 'home',
however, and was careful to take stock of exactly
where I was, even going so far as to count the number
of roads I crossed. There wasn't a human being in
sight. It was a rural area and the houses lining the
road were smaller and poorer-looking than the
Murphys'. Most of them appeared to be small trailers
with the paint peeling off. The tiny gardens
surrounding them were overflowing with rubbish:
plastic bags and bottles by the dozen, along with all
kinds of household junk. It looked like the aftermath of
a violent storm.

A little later that same day Helen went off to
have a lie-down. Jane had already returned home. She
lived in a small town some distance away; Grace was
more or less her nearest neighbour. I was told that

Jane would be back in a day or two. I was pleased at that: there were so many questions I was dying to ask.

Stella and I talked about all sorts of things, some deadly serious, others more lighthearted. On this particular occasion we discussed the role of the media in the terrible chain of events that had brought me to Hugo in the first place. In Stella's opinion, hardly anyone in the US cared a jot about capital punishment; the few who did, and campaigned against it, were for the most part Amnesty and relatives of men and women under sentence of death. 'The majority couldn't care less,' Stella said, a note of bitterness in her voice, 'though if you asked them what if it were *their* son, you might get a very different answer.'

Stella was also convinced that there was widespread corruption in American officialdom. She told me a story about the son of a Texan sheriff who had murdered someone but was never brought to book.

There was nothing I could say in response. I knew too little of such matters. What is more, I wasn't even sure that the story was true; for all I knew, it could have been nothing more than an urban myth. Myth or not, Stella firmly believed it.

Stella had lost many teeth in her lower jaw and her husband's teeth also left much to be desired.

Neither of them could afford to go to a dentist. The medicine Stella took for her heart trouble cost $60 a month and to add to the couple's woes, one of the Pekinese that were under our feet all day long had recently been operated on for a kidney stone, and that had set them back a further $370.

A little later Stella produced an Indian trinket made of artificial pearls; dangling it from her long-nailed fingers, she casually informed me that it had been made by a serial killer. She never wore it, she said, but she had kept it because it had been given her by Pee-Wee.

I asked her if she had been in touch with any other organizations, apart from Amnesty, only to be told that she had tried everything.

'It can take up to fifteen years before they execute him,' she said ruefully. 'I can't bear to think about it.'

She went on to tell me something that had never crossed my mind until that moment, but which I was to hear repeated several times in the future: 'The jury was out for many hours before they delivered their verdict. First for twelve hours to decide on the question of guilt, then for sixteen hours to determine what the sentence should be.'

Like everyone else in the family, Stella steadfastly refused to believe that Pee-Wee had himself killed Lula Mae Denning, but she admitted that he might know something he was unwilling to reveal.

I thought to myself that it could have been his having been an accessory to murder; that would have been almost as serious a crime.

One morning, two letters arrived from Pee-Wee, one for Stella and one for me:

As I write this letter you are in the air on your way to meet my family. I bet you are kind of nervous at the moment, huh? Wondering what it will be like and all. I hope you will have a safe trip and fully enjoy yourself in Oklahoma. I'm sure your stay will be a great one and I hope you will get to take in all the sights that you want to.

He went on to say that he hoped I liked Mississippi Mud Pie and that he had begun to study law. This was news to Stella, and she broke into a broad smile, thinking that it might help him to get his case reviewed.

We had agreed that after three days with Pee-Wee's family, his mother, Grace and her son would drive me to the Greyhound stop, a service station some miles to the south in a small town by the name of Durant.

It was sad saying goodbye to them all, to Pee-Wee's gentlemanly father and to Grandma Helen, who everyone called Mama and who had always treated me with more reserve than the rest of the family. I found out why when I happened to hear her talking in the next room one morning: 'Why should we trust her?' she wanted to know. 'Coming from so far away, we know nothing at all about her. What can *she* do for Pee-Wee that no one else has been able to do?'

I heard Stella defending me, but at the same time I could understand why Helen was so sceptical.

I consoled myself with the thought that Ivan had told me that everyone at the nursing home had been happy to meet me.

On the way to the bus stop Stella and I talked a little about the book I was planning to write. It was she who broached the subject by asking somewhat diffidently if I thought anything would come of it. All I could say in reply was that I would do my best, though I felt compelled to add that I did not know if – or when – I could set about writing it.

To change the subject, I asked her what she thought about the execution, which was set for February.

In reply she simply reiterated her belief that she didn't think anything would come of it. 'It's their way of prolonging the agony, to break the prisoners' morale,' she said. 'They set a date, then they purposely postpone it.'

Stella was proud of her son for trying so hard to get his case reopened, not least because she was convinced that the defence hadn't done a good enough job. I learned that prisoners were entitled to demand a new lawyer if they were dissatisfied with the one they'd been allocated, and that Pee-Wee had twice taken advantage of this right and tried to change his lawyer. He had now been assigned a new defence lawyer and his mother fervently hoped that this one would prove to be a better choice.

Stella sighed heavily. 'I trust that he'll be acquitted one day,' she said.

It was quite a wrench saying goodbye to Stella, her daughter and grandson an hour or so later at the service station in Durant, where I was to catch my bus to Dallas. I'd grown very fond of Stella in the short time we'd been together and I sensed that she felt the same about me. We embraced warmly and vowed to keep in touch.

THE ATLANTA ATTORNEYS

I was picked up at Atlanta Airport by my grandson's American grandparents Ann and Richard. Our grandson was born in the summer of 1991, but a year later his parents divorced. Fortunately, their break-up notwithstanding, both they and their son's grandparents on both sides of the Atlantic remained friends. Richard was a partner in a firm of lawyers while Ann had once been an assistant teacher at a primary school, though that had been many years ago. Jan was both our and their first grandchild.

Following my brief stay in Oklahoma, I had planned to celebrate Thanksgiving with our son's newly acquired family before returning to Norway. It was only then, in the car, on our way to Ann and Richard's spacious house in Buckhead, with its swimming pool and outdoor jacuzzi, that I told my hosts that I had actually come straight from Oklahoma. This was the first they had heard of my friendship with Pee-Wee and my abortive plan to visit him in prison.

On arrival I was treated to a welcome drink and we sat chatting happily together, as people do when they first meet.

To my surprise, an hour or so later we were interrupted by the arrival of a group of Richard's

friends, they too lawyers. I realized at once that he
must have alerted them to my presence without my
knowledge.

Ann and Richard had clearly been taken
aback by what I had told them about my
correspondence with Pee-Wee. Such relationships
were evidently far removed from their daily round;
none of them had ever been called upon to defend a
person under sentence of death, let alone interviewed
a prisoner on Death Row.

Richard himself opened the proceedings.

'I'm truly impressed,' he said, 'and I greatly
appreciate what you are doing. But you realize, I'm
sure, that he's guilty. It's obvious that he's repressed
the memory of what he's done, but that doesn't mean
that he shouldn't pay for it, even if it's years before he
does. There'll be all those appeals to go through first.'

Shocked to the core, I somehow managed to
stammer out:

'Do you mean to say that you're in favour of
capital punishment?'

'Of course I am,' Richard replied. He raised
his glass and gave me a pitying smile. 'One hundred
per cent.'

Lost for words, I simply stared at him.

He gestured towards the others. 'So are they.
Just ask them.'

He was right. His friends did all they could to
convince me that they were of the same opinion. To
make sure that I understood why, gently but firmly

they began to recall murder cases they had either read
of or heard about. I was even more surprised to find
hat not one of them was opposed to the death penalty.
I learned that even the defence lawyers among them
were of the same mind. They pointed out that
nowhere in the civilized world were more appalling
crimes committed than in the United States. In return
I did my best to get them to see things my way, citing
the country's notoriously lax gun laws and pointing
out that it was very much a matter of chance who
received a death sentence and who got away with
imprisonment for life – or, in some cases, if they
happened to have a particularly smart defence
counsel, got off scot free. It was to no avail: they
wouldn't budge an inch. The following week I found
to my astonishment that 80 per cent of Americans
were in agreement with Richard's diehard
colleagues.[12]

Pee-Wee knew all about my visit to Georgia's capital
city, which explains why he had begun to read all he
could about what was happening in the state. He told
me that the authorities had begun discussions on an
even more inhumane method of execution, which only
served to add to my despondency. Because of my
family connections, I felt warmly disposed towards the
state. One of my favourite songs was, in fact, Hoagy
Carmichael's 'Georgia on my Mind' with lyrics by
Stuart Gorrell.

> I have heard that the state of Georgia wants to
> bring back the gallows, that way they can use
> the organs of the people that they said they
> wasn't worth to live in this society.

In the event, only one person was executed in Georgia
that year (1994); on the other hand, an additional 30
were executed in the rest of the country, 14 of them in
Texas.[13]

SUSPENSE

Awaiting me on my return to Norway was a letter
from Pee-Wee to say how glad he was that I had been
to visit his parents and asking to know more about
how we had got on. In return I sent him a batch of
photographs I had taken of his family and friends.

A month before I set off for Oklahoma, Pee-Wee's
application to the Supreme Court of Texas to have his
case reviewed once again had been turned down. That
was why the date set for his execution had been
rescheduled for February. An appeal to the Supreme
Court for a review of a decision handed down by a
lower court is a course open to everyone under
sentence of death and something a prisoner can avail
himself of repeatedly if there appear to be reasonable
grounds for doing so.[14] At the same time prisoners
may have their cases reviewed in a lower, federal
court, as Pee-Wee was able to do.

In a letter dated 7 January 1995 Pee-Wee wrote:

> I have not been feeling very well lately. I don't
> know if you know, but I have a[n] execution
> date, I had gotten it before you had came to
> the states, but I didn't want to ruin your trip
> with the news. I have filed motions for a stay

of execution and for a lawyer, but as I write
this letter I haven't received any news on that
yet. [...] I've not said probably 30 words to
anyone since I received that date. [...] I
haven't even told my parents about the date.

Pee-Wee had no idea that Stella had already told me
of the date set for his execution. As it happens, I would
have known it anyway, had I taken the trouble to read
through the copy of the official order for his execution
Stella had sent me. Pee-Wee had himself received a
copy on 9 November 1994, along with notification,
couched in cold, dispassionate legalese not unlike a
pre-operative briefing, that, a few hours before dawn
on 16 February 1995, he would be transferred to a
room in The Walls where, before the sun had set, he
would be strapped down and given a lethal injection.
There he would be left until certified dead by two
suitably qualified officials.

The letter was signed by none other than Ray
F. Grisham, the judge who had handed down the
original sentence.

Thanks to the many opportunities open to him
to lodge an appeal and the time taken by the Supreme
Court to come to a decision, four long years had
elapsed from the day Pee-Wee was first sentenced to
death until a date was finally set for his execution.

Immediately upon receipt of Pee-Wee's letter,
I faxed him via Ellis Unit 1 to let him know that I was
aware that he was due to be executed on 16 February.
I also wrote that I had learned from his mother that

he had been allotted a new attorney and asked him to
let me have the man's name and phone and fax
numbers. As a precaution, I had earlier phoned the
Prison Governor's office about faxing Pee-Wee, only
to be informed that they couldn't guarantee that he
would ever receive what I sent, but that I was at
liberty to try.

Two days after receiving my fax Pee-Wee
wrote again and told me off in no uncertain terms. He
was very put out at what I had done and wanted me to
promise never to fax the prison again. It appeared that
he had been instructed to inform me that fax
communication was for administrative purposes only
and that prisoners were not allowed such privileges.
He also said that he was going to return the US
stamps I had sent him from Atlanta, as he was not
allowed to have them. What is more, he made no
attempt to hide his annoyance at the fact that, because
of my fax, it was now common knowledge among his
fellow prisoners that a date had been set for his
execution. He himself had told no one, but now
everyone was talking about it.

Despite the rumpus it had caused, never for a
moment did I regret sending that fax. On reflection,
however, when I learned that Pee-Wee had himself
never told anyone of the date set for his execution, not
even members of his own family, I realized that his
anguish must have been well-nigh unbearable.

I really don't know what to say right now. I
have so many things going through my head.

I haven't heard from my mother in a while,
she was supposed to come visiting me this
month, but I haven't seen her yet. [. . .] I don't
live the way others do. I live for today and not
[to]morrow. [. . .] I have learned over the
years that if you let your mind control your
thoughts you will not be happy, and that is
how it will be now and if tomorrow comes it
will be the same.

In January 1995 I phoned Stella. She told me that Pee-Wee had been very active as the date set for his execution drew closer. He had immersed himself in a study of the law and was constantly finding new snippets of information he thought might help his case. He was also doing all he could to get the execution postponed, writing to public officials in an endeavour to convince them that he had not received fair treatment – that he had been adjudged guilty before the trial even started and that the court proceedings had not been according to the book.

Stella had recently had a spell in hospital with pneumonia. I urged her to start wearing socks, but she said she couldn't stand socks and preferred to go barefooted. I joked that it was the Indian blood in her veins, which made her laugh.

On 12 January I wrote Pee-Wee to say that I was trying to enlist the aid of the Norwegian Amnesty representative, to see if we could bring his case to the notice of an international public. He made no comment but wrote instead:

My family think the world of you. Besides, if
any of my family would have said anything
bad about you I would never speak to them
again, but my mother and father welcome you
in their home any time you are here.

In my reply I said that I would like to visit him and
asked him to keep me on his visitors list. He had put
me on it when he learned that I was going to
Oklahoma.

Drawing made by Pee-Wee

POSTPONED – AGAIN

Towards the end of January 1995 Pee-Wee wrote to say that he had been granted another stay of execution. 'That took a load off my shoulders,' he said.

This postponement resulted from Pee-Wee's own efforts. As soon as he was informed that a date had been set for his execution, as was customary with prisoners in his position he had submitted an appeal. This led to a second postponement and meant that a new execution date could not be set until his appeal had been heard. In effect, he had bought himself extra time.

On the whole, Pee-Wee remained optimistic. He hoped – and believed – that even if his appeal were denied, next time around he would be met with the realization that the time had come to reappraise his case. He had great confidence in the new attorney he had recently been allocated.

> 15 April 1995:
> My new lawyer came to talk to me a few weeks ago and he talked very positive about helping get me a new trial. It's very complicated to explain to you in order not to get you confused about the appeal process.

I'll just say that during each step of the appeal, any lawyer I do get will try to get me a new trial.

Pee-Wee's new lawyer had admitted to him that he had never defended a person under sentence of death before. Pee-Wee himself said that the man seemed to be in doubt about a lot of things but that he liked him for all of that. The new lawyer had taken his wife along to their first meeting and Pee-Wee said he had taken a liking to her, too.

By this time the heat of summer had returned, forcing Pee-Wee to do all he could not to over-exert himself.

In writing to me he constantly returned to the man he referred to as the 'false witness', the man who had testified against him in court. He insisted that he had never even met the man until he heard him give evidence at the trial.

8 June 1995:
I am on Death Row because a person said I confessed to him about this crime and I NEVER SPOKE TO THAT GUY AND I DON'T EVEN KNOW HIM, so if I don't trust anyone here and talk to them, they can't go and say I said something to them that I didn't.

I still meditate every day for it is the only thing in my life that helps me stay sane. I look within to find love and peace. I used to go fishing as much as I could, I would walk

through the woods as much as I could,
because the trees give off so much energy and
they also put off oxygen and without them
everything around us would die off.

Pee-Wee often told me that his dearest wish was once again to be able to walk bare-footed through lush green grass, something he had not done for many years. That, he said, was one of life's small joys people outside the prison walls took for granted. He maintained that what he wanted more than anything else was to help young people. In one of his letters he told me that he had once borrowed a small fishing boat, which he enjoyed very much.

In August 1995 he had seen on television a Norwegian sprinter, Geir Moen, run in a 200-metre race at Oslo's Bislet Stadium and he wanted to know how far away from the stadium I lived and if I'd ever been there. I replied that I wasn't particularly interested in sport, though I had been to Bislet quite a number of times.

I asked him if he would consider being my illustrator if ever I published another book; without hesitation he said yes. Shortly afterwards he came up with a whole string of ideas for a new children's book of his own, one of them centring on a married couple who died in an accident. They had three children and it fell to the oldest, who was fifteen, to look after her younger brother and sister. The three children found themselves living more or less on the streets and finding it hard to survive. The only thing that kept them going was their shared dream of a better life.

The book Pee-Wee envisaged writing would be about loyalty, courage in adversity, sticking together, strength of character and the ability to tackle the problems of daily life without parental support. He had plans for a second book, too, and then a third, all equally imaginative and original.

KORINNA, A BOLT
FROM THE BLUE

When I first started writing to Pee-Wee, I assumed
that I was his one and only pen-friend, but after we
had been corresponding for some two years or more I
discovered that there were others as well who were as
concerned about his plight as I was. To be fair, in an
earlier letter he *had* once made passing reference to a
certain Korinna Hofheinz, a Swiss medical student
who had visited him in prison. It transpired that
Korinna had entered his life only a few months after I
myself had become acquainted with him through
Amnesty. Korinna was closer to Pee-Wee's own age
and he had confided in me that he rather liked her
and that she was cheerful and good fun – a little too
wrapped up in herself, he thought, but pleasant with
it. Almost as an afterthought, he had added that she
was forever changing boyfriends.

In time I discovered that he had even more
pen friends, though Korinna and myself seemed to be
those he felt closest to. For reasons best known to
himself, Pee-Wee never mentioned the other people
he corresponded with. Whatever the reason, I was
relieved to know that he was in touch with others
besides me, as that meant that I wasn't the only one he
was always looking forward to receiving a letter from.

I had always felt duty-bound to write frequently to
him, but finding the time to do so wasn't always easy.

It was evident that he had told Korinna about
his correspondence with me as, on 15 August 1995,
almost a year after I had been to stay with Stella,
Korinna wrote her initial letter to me: 'You may not
know about me, but I know a lot about you.'

By the time her letter reached me she had
already visited Pee-Wee twice and his parents once.
She said she was very happy that Pee-Wee and I had
become friends and that 'someone like me had entered
his life'.

I learned that Korinna had spent a few
pleasant days with Pee-Wee's parents in Hugo and
that she had also had some rewarding conversations
with him in prison. She confessed that she often felt
both sad and helpless when she allowed herself to
think about what the future held in store for him.

Korinna firmly believed that Pee-Wee was
innocent. She had read all the relevant documents and
discovered that much of the evidence against him was
flawed. She earnestly wished that she could do more
to help but consoled herself with the thought that her
friendship was also of benefit to him.

'He has lived a chequered life,' she wrote, 'but
he's a wonderful person, he really is.' I found it
comforting to know that I wasn't the only one who
saw him in that light.

It was Stella who had given Korinna my
address and told her that I was planning a trip to

Huntsville to see Pee-Wee. Korinna strongly encouraged me to put my plan into effect and offered a few practical hints based on her own visits to Huntsville. She also told me how her own friendship with Pee-Wee had progressed and that she had taken every opportunity to become better acquainted with him from the moment she was first invited to become a pen friend.

At this point something occurred that I found very hard to understand. Pee-Wee was furious at what he saw as Korinna's temerity in contacting me and he was even angrier when he realized that it was Stella who had brought us together. He was going to 'have it out' with his mother for that, he wrote. He greatly disliked the fact that the two had – in his eyes – gone behind his back the way they had.

I had never known Pee-Wee so worked up about anything before. This was a very different Pee-Wee from the one I thought I knew. In our innocence, had Korinna and I allowed ourselves to be deceived? I began to ask myself just who Pee-Wee was. In my reply I told him to calm down and did my best to justify what the three of us had done. I also tried to convince him that it was to his advantage that we were in touch with each other and thus able to cooperate in helping him. After a while he began to see it our way and to come to terms with the situation.

In time I came to realize that none of the inmates liked their friends outside the prison talking together and collaborating on their behalf. It seemed that they preferred to have each of their correspondents wholly to themselves and were unwilling to share them with others.

I later learned from other visitors that this was a widespread reaction among prisoners on Death Row.

On 1 October 1995 I received another letter from Korinna. 'I'm sorry that I surprised you by writing to you like that. Pee-Wee was angry with me because he was afraid you would think he had given me your address without your permission. He would never have done that. I got it from Stella when I was there. I promised Ivan that I would write to you and explain how it all came about. He has a strong sense of justice and was afraid that my action might have led you to believe that he had abused your trust in him by going behind your back.'

In time Korinna and I became good friends and Pee-Wee gradually came to understand the benefits that accrued from our friendship.

That year, 1995, 56 prisoners under sentence of death in the US, were executed, 19 of them in Texas.[15]

EN ROUTE TO ELLIS UNIT 1

I have a feeling that many things will happen
in my life this year, and they will all be good.
My case will be resolved, and I will then be
released, because of the false accusations
against me. I will talk more about this when
you arrive next month. I am looking forward
to seeing you.

March 1996 – and at long last I was getting ready for
my trip to Huntsville to visit Pee-Wee. By then we had
already exchanged more than thirty letters and we
both felt that the time had come to meet. As I had last
time, I planned to carry on to Atlanta afterwards.

I was the only passenger to disembark at the
Greyhound terminal in Huntsville when the coach
pulled in at eight in the evening. I had boarded it four
hours earlier in Dallas, my only luggage a carry-on
bag with a few bare necessities; I had left my suitcase,
which was full of presents for my family, back at the
hotel in Dallas.

It was already dark, the terminal was closed
and there wasn't a soul in sight apart from people
waiting for transport to their final destinations.

At a loss, I asked the driver of my coach what
he thought I should do. His only suggestion was that I

should phone for a taxi. Then, without more ado, he let in the clutch and the Greyhound coach, with all it meant in terms of comfort and security, disappeared round the corner of the building, leaving me feeling very much alone.

I couldn't help but feel a trifle uneasy. I followed round the corner of the terminal until, in a niche, I eventually came across a public telephone affixed to the wall. It was so dark that I only spotted it thanks to the lights of passing cars. Brightened only by a few lack-lustre graffiti, on that bare wall it looked very forlorn and uninviting, but at least it was a phone. I looked about me: the street was deserted.

There was a strong wind blowing and the air was filled with the creaking of rusty metal signs, while the empty street was littered with scraps of paper and other refuse picked up by the wind. I heard the sound of an approaching car, then a small pick-up drew into the kerb behind me. I turned away from it but I could feel the driver's gaze boring into my back as I tried desperately to get through to someone on the phone. There wasn't a number there to help me – nothing, just a blank wall. I tried hard to suppress my rising panic. Here I was, I thought, alone and defenceless in a strange town and with a man in a darkened car only a short distance away.

In desperation I did what people do in films: I dialled 00 and asked for the operator. How welcome and reassuring the calm voice of the woman who answered was. 'What can I do for you, ma'am?' she asked politely. I implored her to help me find a cab, only to be told that she couldn't, as she knew nothing about taxi companies where I was.

Stella had told me that in America there were always taxis waiting outside bus stations, but here in Huntsville there were none at all. She had also warned me not to try walking to my hotel, as it was far too dangerous. On the coach I had read and reread Korinna's letter telling me about all the formalities I would have to go through before I got to see Pee-Wee, but I wouldn't need that information, useful though it was, until the following day. She didn't say anything that would help me in my present predicament.

After a while the operator seemed to have grasped how desperate I was and gave me the number of the local police station – just in time, it seemed, as at that moment the driver of the pickup switched off his engine. I rang the police and they put me in touch with a taxi driver, who promised to come as soon as he could. I was debating with myself whether to tell the police about the car standing behind me at the kerb when, to my great relief, the driver restarted his engine and drove off.

Twenty minutes were to pass before the taxi came. In the meantime I wandered restlessly around the deserted bus terminal. I thought the passing cars were stopping while their drivers sized me up until I realized that, coming as they were from a side road, at the crossroads they were compelled by law to do so.

The thought struck me that I was at a crossroads myself: the following day I was destined to meet a man under sentence of death, a man with whom I had been corresponding for over three years.

When at long last the taxi arrived, the driver apologized profusely for the delay. He explained that the number of the taxi company was normally to be found on the wall beside the phone but that it was constantly being vandalized and pulled down.

I eventually reached my destination, Hospitality House, only to discover to my chagrin that it was no more than a stone's throw from the bus terminal; I could have walked there in under two minutes. I rang the bell of a modern-looking building set amid well-kept lawns and flowerbeds.

The door was opened by a burly, pleasant-looking man in his fifties or sixties who introduced himself as Bob. He told me that he ran the guesthouse, which catered to the needs of families and friends visiting inmates of the nearby prison, with the aid of his wife and another woman, Betty. All three were Baptists, the guesthouse being funded by the Baptist church.[16] There was no charge for accommodation but visitors who were in a position to do so were expected to make a small contribution towards running costs. Before being allotted a room, I had to fill in a form and state the name of the prisoner I was visiting. I was handed a set of newly laundered bed linen and informed that Hospitality House was self-catering throughout. Bob then showed me to my room, which, though sparsely furnished, was spotlessly clean and tidy.

There was a crocheted quilt on the bed but only one light, and that was in the ceiling. The solitary window was set high up in the wall with, beneath it, a large bookcase completely bare of books. The kitchen turned out to be large and airy and all the cupboards were stacked high with cans of food, mainly stews and soups.

'Just help yourself to whatever you want,' Bob said. 'All I do is make the morning coffee. You'll have to get your own breakfast.'

Later that same evening I made the acquaintance of Hal from California. Bob had told me a little about him before he retired for the night.

'He's been here for a couple of days now,' he said. 'His son is on Death Row. He'll give you a lift to the prison, I'm sure. He's gone to a meeting but he'll be back soon.'

I was glad to hear about the chance of a lift, as it would save me the expense of a taxi, but I didn't relish the thought of driving to the prison with an unknown man. Ellis Unit 1, where both Pee-Wee and Hal's son were held, was some six miles from downtown Huntsville. But who was Hal exactly? Bob had said nothing to enlighten me. Did I dare sit in a car with a complete stranger, a man who, moreover, was the father of someone condemned to death for murder? I understood that Bob trusted him but I was also well aware that he didn't know Hal much better than I did, as it was the first time he had stayed at Hospitality House. I decided that the wisest course

98

was to wait until I had met the man and had a chance
to weigh him up.

Hal turned out to be an affable-looking man; I guessed
his age at between sixty and seventy. With his bald
head, and with a large gold ring in his left ear, he
looked like a onetime prize fighter. He was wearing
loose-fitting shorts and a white T-shirt with ST
OLAV'S COLLEGE MINNESOTA emblazoned on
the front above his bulging paunch. Behind his over-
large, gold-framed spectacles his eyes had an impish
glint.

    Smiling, he stretched out a hand and said in
Norwegian: 'Good evening, Marit. So you're from
Norway. My grandparents were Norwegian.' It later
transpired that that was all the Norwegian he knew.

    Hal was clearly at home in the kitchen, as he
strode across to the refrigerator and took out two cans
of coke. Handing one to me, he ushered me into the
day room, where he began to tell me what had
brought him to Huntsville.

    He said that twelve years ago his only son,
Randall, had been standing with his Harley Davidson
beside the road when a policeman stopped his car and
came over to ask to see his licence. As the man was in
civilian clothes and driving an ordinary car, Randall
hadn't realized that he was a police officer. Fearing
that he was about to be robbed, he had drawn a gun
and the policeman had done the same. High on drugs
at the time, Randall had fired before the policeman

had had a chance to identify himself, killing him on the spot. Randall was sentenced to death and had been trying for years to get his case reviewed, but without success. He had done his utmost to convince the authorities that he sincerely regretted what he had done, that it had all been a misunderstanding, that he had thought he was acting in self-defence and had panicked. All he wanted was to be given a chance to begin a new life and redeem himself.

When I met Hal, Randall was forty-two years old. At the time of the shooting he had had a wife and children, but he was no longer in touch with any of them. Nor was his father, but he did know that he had five grandchildren and one great-grandchild. Randall's ex-wife had advised them to forget both him and his family. I could see the tears in Hal's eyes as he spoke.

'I didn't think it right that I shouldn't be allowed to see my own grandchildren,' Hal said. His voice grew bitter. 'I miss them more than I can say, just as I do my son. It's not only the perpetrator who suffers when someone's executed, it's his entire family.'

Stella and Jane had both said the same thing.

'In this country, killing a police officer is the worst crime of all,' Hal continued. He shook his head sadly. 'Sentencing people to death for it is well-established policy, it's almost mandatory. They execute far too many people in America. Four people were put to death in December alone – execution is big business. In Texas, more than 80 per cent of the population are in favour of the death penalty. It's one of the worst states in the country in that respect. Governors are elected according to whether or not they are for the death penalty.'

The longer we conversed, the more Hal opened up.

'I divorced when my son was still small. I've been a very poor father. In those days I was an alcoholic, but I haven't touched alcohol for eight years now.'

I learned that the reason Hal had been so late getting back to Hospitality House the previous evening was because he had been at a meeting of the local branch of Alcoholics Anonymous. It transpired that this was something he did whenever he came to Huntsville. He said that for him the best part of these meetings was when there were newcomers present – it made him feel that he had a mission in life. He drew on his own experience to prove to them that the solution was to renounce alcohol altogether.

'When I stopped drinking,' he said, 'I lost over a hundred pounds.' It was then I understood why he had such a shambling, hangdog air about him and was so bowed and gaunt. Having so much less excess weight to carry around made it easier for him to bear a different kind of burden, that of having his only son in prison awaiting execution.

Hal told me about something that had made a vivid impression on him the first time he had visited his son in Huntsville. A prisoner had been executed the day he arrived and in the evening a large crowd of people had gathered outside The Walls to 'celebrate' the event. People laughed and cheered when it was officially announced that the execution had been successfully carried out. 'They staged an impromptu barbecue out there in the street and gorged themselves on T-bone steaks,' Hal said. 'I've never forgotten it and never will. That was when I cut out drinking.'

He shuddered at the thought.

'Standing in silence on the other side of the street were representatives of Amnesty carrying flaming torches. There were people from the Christian churches there too, singing hymns.'

I ventured to ask him if there was any hope of a reprieve for his son.

'Well,' he replied, 'there's always a hope that a death sentence will be commuted to life, but I don't think there's any chance of that for my son.'

He regretted that he was unable to help his son financially. There had been a time when he'd been quite comfortably off, but now he was virtually destitute.

'I've lost everything I ever had.' The admission came easily to his lips.

I gathered that most of Hal's money had been spent on drink; the rest had gone on legal fees in a vain attempt to get his son reprieved. When I met Hal, the only way he could help his son was to visit him three times a year. He drove in his old wreck of a car all the way from California to Huntsville. It was a two-day drive at best and he had to sleep in the car as he couldn't afford a motel.

'Tomorrow's my third and last day,' Hal said. 'I'll be off in the morning, as soon as I've seen my son.'

We agreed to set off together for Ellis Unit at seven the following day as Hal knew from experience that it could be difficult to get to see a prisoner later in the day.

My head was still in a whirl when, at long last, I got to bed; it took me quite a while to fall asleep.

***

I awoke next morning to the delicious aroma of freshly made coffee. Hal was already up and about when I entered the day room, where we were joined by Bob, who told us something about Hospitality House.

I learned that they'd had several thousand visitors since they opened nine years earlier. A stack of well-filled guest books testified to how grateful these visitors had been. I leafed through two or three of the books and read what people had written in appreciation. Bob and his wife and Betty had always been there, ready to help and provide solace to those in need. Korinna had referred to them as 'three true angels right here on God's earth'. She had grown very attached to them in the course of the four days she had spent in their company. In her last letter to me she had asked to be remembered to them. This seemed to be a good time to do so, and when I passed on her greeting, Bob remembered her immediately, not least because of her flaming red hair. I had never met her, of course, but I found it easy to visualize what she looked like when he described her. Bob said there were a lot of people who felt a need for comfort and that he spent a lot of time consoling prisoners' grieving mothers and sisters, especially immediately prior to and following an execution.

I was told that few fathers came to visit their erring sons. I was reminded of Pee-Wee's father, who could never bring himself to visit his son and never said a word about what had happened to him. He had lost his job when Pee-Wee was sentenced to death and shortly afterwards suffered a severe heart attack from which he had still not wholly recovered. He had finally bowed to the inevitable, however, and occasionally even managed to talk about it, despite the emotional strain involved.

Bob and Hal were saddened by the attitude taken by so many of their fellow countrymen. Bob sincerely hoped that one day they would come round and see things in a different light. His dearest wish was to live long enough to see this happen but he was realistic enough to acknowledge that the chances were slim. More people than usual had, in fact, been recently executed in Texas and another execution – of a Mexican – was scheduled for the following day. A last appeal for a stay of execution or a pardon had been lodged with the governor, who had the final word, but time was running out and there had been no response.

I took the opportunity to take a closer look at the day room; I hadn't had time the previous evening as I had spent it talking to Hal. Large and airy, it was full of old-fashioned armchairs grouped around sturdy looking tables. Lying on one table was a partly completed jigsaw puzzle, a scene from the classic fairy tale of the Sleeping Beauty. I surmised that it had helped to take people's minds off the reason for their visit, but couldn't help but wonder how many hands had sorted through the pieces and whether it would ever be finished.

The end wall was devoted to photographs of prisoners who had been executed, newspaper cuttings and soberly worded official announcements that such-and-such a prisoner had been executed. There were also some emotionally charged verses written by prisoners and bereaved mothers, sisters and children. My eye was caught by a large black-and-white photograph of a sweet-looking boy in a striped jersey playing alone without a care in the world. I learned that when he grew to manhood he'd committed murder and been put to death.

Hal and I were still the only ones staying at Hospitality House when, at seven o'clock the same morning, we set off in his rusty old car. Hal apologized for the fact that the door couldn't be opened on the passenger's side. He said that a vagrant begging for a handout had taken it out on the nearside fender when Hal told him he was broke. Hal shrugged it off with the remark that it was a pity, as it would never be repaired.

When we turned right at the end of the drive I caught sight of the bus station where, only the day before, I had felt so scared and vulnerable as I stood waiting for the taxi; now it looked very prosaic and not the least bit threatening.

Hal stopped off at a nearby shop to buy doughnuts. He came back with a bulging bag that must have contained twenty at least. He invited me to help myself, even though they were meant to last him all the way back to California later in the day. He talked nonstop as he drove: 'I've lived a really harum-scarum kind of life,' he said.

He talked fast and laughter came easily to him. It was his sense of humour, he said, that had carried him through. He had a habit of shrugging his shoulders every now and then as if to say that nothing mattered now, anyway.

I hoped with all my heart that from now on things would go better for him. He told me that when he was younger he had been much in demand as a hairdresser in Hollywood and had been close friends with some of the stars, most notably June Allyson. I remembered June Allyson very well: as a star-struck child, I had written to her and received an autographed photograph in return.

Thanks to Hal I was able to remain reasonably calm throughout my first scary encounter with Ellis Unit. I had been given permission to spend two successive days with Pee-Wee – from eight to twelve in the morning. Korinna had warned me that we would have to converse through a glass partition. 'He'll be

106

sitting in a cage, yes, really, a cage inside a cage,' was how she put it.

Hal, who knew the prison routine inside-out, prepared me for what lay ahead. Korinna had also done her best to prime me, but I was glad to have a real live human being beside me to help me face the ordeal.

I took my handbag with me when I got out of the car but to my dismay was told that visitors were not allowed to take personal belongings into the prison. An exception was made in my case for my passport and return air ticket to Norway, which I had to show because I was there on what was classed as a 'special visit'. I was allowed to keep a little small change. Hal said I could leave my handbag, which contained my credit cards and other valuables, in his car. I was very grateful at the time, though when I told my friends back in Norway about what I had done, they were horrified. They couldn't understand how I could have trusted a man who was to all intents and purposes a complete stranger.

At the entrance to the prison we got talking to a woman who introduced herself as Betty and said that she was a prison visitor. I judged her to be in her fifties. Betty was together with another woman, Valerie – or Vi, as Betty called her – from Ireland. Vi and I were both about the same age as Betty but, unlike her, were corresponding with only one prisoner. Hal had told me that Vi was in the habit of writing personal poems, which she placed in the grave whenever she attended a prisoner's funeral. When she heard that I had come all the way from Norway, she exclaimed: 'Your friend's a very lucky man. There are many in here who never receive a visit from anyone.'

Just outside the gate stood a tall watchtower manned by a woman prison officer. One after the other, we had to shout up to her the number of the prisoner we were visiting. All visits had been approved in advance and for one terrifying moment I was afraid that I had given her the wrong number. My fears proved groundless, however, as she dutifully lowered a plastic bucket on a cord into which I had to place my identification documents, which she then hoisted up to check.

'She won't hesitate to fire if something untoward happens,' Hal warned me.

A few minutes later the bucket came down again, together with my passport and return ticket, and the first gate clicked open. The assembled visitors, some fifteen in all, were sluiced through a succession of similar gates, each of which clicked open automatically when the one behind us clicked shut – but not before.

Once inside, we were checked again, this time by a woman securely ensconced behind a sturdy-looking counter where, one at a time, we had to sign ourselves in and I had to hand in my passport and return ticket. All she said was that I was to take seat No. 19. There wasn't a hint of a smile from any of the prison staff – a striking contrast to the many friendly Americans I had met elsewhere.

My head was spinning, but fortunately Hal realized
that it was all getting to be a bit too much for me and
pointed out the rest room and a machine dispensing
soft drinks and snacks. Then he showed me
to my seat, a hard and Spartan-looking spindle-back
chair on which I was expected to perch for the next
four hours. It was icy-cold in the room and I regretted
not having brought warmer clothes.

The prisoners' area was in the shape of a
horseshoe in the middle of the room. Visitors had to
sit side by side in a ring round it. The men they had
come to visit sat opposite them, each in a separate
cubicle; between prisoner and visitor was a thick pane
of glass with a grille at the bottom through which they
could converse.

When we were all in our places outside the
glass partition, the prisoners were brought in, one by
one. As each and every one was brought in by the
same officer, it goes without saying that it took an
interminably long time before they were all in their
allotted places. I had no idea of when it would be Pee-
Wee's turn to be collected.

With nothing to do but wait, I glanced about
me at the other visitors. Betty and Vi were seated on
the two chairs to my right. On my left were a Mexican
woman and a number of blacks and whites. Hal apart,
as far as I could see there was only one man among
them.

Hal had told me that one of the women from
Europe had fallen deeply in love with her prisoner;

what is more, she had sold her house to set up a fund to pay for his defence. I couldn't help but wonder who this woman could be, and eventually came to the conclusion that it had to be the elegantly clad, distinguished-looking, white-haired lady sitting directly across from me.

Hal had shaken his head at her naiveté. 'There isn't a hope for any of them,' he said sadly. He didn't think any of these 'special' prisoners would ever be released, no matter how proficient the lawyers their sponsors retained for them.

Hal waved to me through the glass partition while he waited for his son to be brought in. He had sat there time and time again over the years, listening to his son's recriminations and disgruntlement with the American government. Hal had seen his own life ruined by the young man's impulsive action. Randall's mother had moved to be nearer to the prison, to enable her to visit her son more often, but for her, too, life had lost all meaning and she was overburdened with sorrow.

My mouth dry, I waited -- and waited -- until my eyes fell on the soft-drinks dispenser behind me. I comforted myself with the thought that I would be able to get both Pee-Wee and myself something to drink to help us through the next few hours. Whatever I bought for him would have to be collected by a guard and delivered to him through a hatch set there for the purpose.

Most of the prisoners were by this time deep in
conversation with their visitors. Wherever I looked
there were women – smiling, laughing, chatting avidly
away or shaking their heads in despair.

And still I waited. My nerves were on edge. I both
dreaded what lay before me and looked forward to it
with no little anticipation. Every now and again a
tremor ran down my spine.

Pee-Wee and I had been corresponding for
three years or more and some forty letters had passed
between us. In a sense, we knew each other well – but
we had never met in person.

Suddenly I realized that the moment had
come. The man approaching me was Pee-Wee!

FACE TO FACE

He was shorter and more thickset than he had
appeared to be in his photographs. He had told me
that he had once been quite slim, but that the prison
food was anything but healthy and far too full of fats
and starch. The result was plain to see.

He was handcuffed, as Korinna had said he
would be, and was accompanied by the same guard as
had brought in the others. He had refused to take part
in the work programme organized by the prison,
preferring, he said, to spend his time on creative
pursuits such as meditation, artwork, drawing and
writing, rather than sitting with a lot of other prisoners
sewing prison uniforms and other simple garments.
Because of his intransience, whenever he was allowed
out of his cell he was handcuffed.[17]

Once in the cage, Pee-Wee turned away from
me and thrust his hands through the hatch for the
guard to remove his handcuffs; the cage was then
locked from the outside.

That done, he sat down facing me. He looked
me straight in the eye. I could see that he had his
father's blue eyes but Stella's colouring and that, taken
all round, he looked very much like her. He had a pale
skin and my eyes were drawn to a white scar above his
upper lip. His long black eyelashes curled upwards

and I saw that what he had once said about people claiming he had a special look in his eyes was true. He had.

Pee-Wee was undeniably a good-looking man. His glance was firm and direct, his eyebrows thick, black and well formed, his close-cropped hair dark brown. He gave me a warm, shy smile.

I was fully aware that at the same time he was sizing me up and that he would later probably give me a detailed account of his first impression of me. I had chosen to wear a simple white blouse buttoned up to the neck and black slacks; shorts were not allowed.

He put his hands on the glass in greeting and I placed my own against his. I noticed that his hands, which looked soft and well cared for, were surprisingly small for a man of his size. The thought struck me that it was those hands that had drawn the lovely little pictures and penned the emotive verses he had sent me.

Could those selfsame hands have actually killed someone? Could this, to my eyes, innocent-looking young man really have battered a defenceless old woman to death? He was universally liked in the prison, I knew, but there was no telling. Was he as nice as he appeared to be? And why couldn't his sentence be commuted to life, at least? What was needed for that? My mind went back to one of the newspaper cuttings relating to the trial that I had read for a second time shortly before I left home.

The defence had called as a witness a certain Ms D.J. Weaver, an expert on alcoholics and drug addicts. She had told the court that Mr Murphy (Pee-Wee was always addressed and referred to by officials as 'Mr') had successfully completed the Alcoholics Anonymous (AA) twelve-part course and in consequence undergone a significant change of personality. She had also said that it was the first time in her entire career as a consultant that she had felt constrained to testify to a prisoner's advantage. In her opinion, Pee-Wee's whole mental outlook had changed since he came under the influence of AA.

She then went on to explain that prisoners were not allowed to participate in an AA course of treatment unless they had expressed a sincere wish to change their ways. She had also emphasized that AA only accepted men who were genuinely interested and determined to turn over a new leaf. In regard to Pee-Wee, she said, 'he was not only a part of the group, he was the best of them and was chosen to head it'. Weaver also told the court that she always looked for honesty and remorse in prisoners attending AA sessions and that she felt that Pee-Wee qualified on both counts. She had seen a transformation in him in that he had accepted responsibility for his misdoings.

Jarvis, the district attorney, had then asked Ms Weaver if there was a cure for dependence on alcohol and drugs. 'Abstention is the closest we can come to a cure,' was her reply. 'One's well-being depends on one's abstaining, day after day, and I feel that Mr Murphy has made that choice. I will stake my reputation and my career on the correctness of that assumption.'

'But no one can guarantee a thing like that,' was
Jarvis's response.'

'No, I don't think they can,' Ms Weaver
replied.

'Tell me, Ms Weaver, has a prisoner ever
managed to deceive you?' was the next question.

'Yes, once or twice,' was the answer.

I couldn't help but wonder if Pee-Wee had
hoodwinked Ms Weaver – or whether, as I hoped, he
really had changed for the better.

Pee-Wee rubbed his eyes. Thanks to the ventilation
slits I had no difficulty in hearing what he said.

'It's great to see you. Did you have a good
trip?' he asked. Before I could answer, he went on to
confess that he had only just woken up.

I'd been afraid I might not understand all he
said, but fortunately he proved easier to follow than
his mother, not least because he spoke more clearly.

When, later on, I was asked how we had managed to
fill our allotted four hours together, all I could say was
that I no longer remembered. We talked about
everything and nothing. It was an emotionally charged
meeting altogether and time simply flew by. We both
cried a little, that I do remember, but we also laughed
a lot. There was something near-magical about it all,
but it seemed a little unreal, too. After all, we had
shared so many thoughts and feelings in our letters
that we not infrequently found ourselves lost for
words. I certainly did. Pee-Wee did most of the

talking, though what he actually thought I have no means of knowing. I was his first visitor for over a year.

I greatly regretted not having been permitted to take in a notebook and pencil. Beside me were two lawyers, both of whom were free to write whatever they wanted; on the other hand, they were allowed only two hours with their clients as opposed to my four. I did my best to commit to memory some of the more pivotal points of our conversation but in vain, not least because Pee-Wee talked so fast that at times I lost track of what he was saying. Worst of all was when he got onto the ever-recurring subject of how he had been 'set up' in court, how poor his lawyers had been, how disappointed he was in them and that he would never, ever give up. He was determined to walk out of Huntsville a free man, after which he intended to come to Norway to visit me and my family. He was looking forward to that, he said. He was also resolved to study, with medicine as his first choice. I don't think I thought much about it at the time, apart from reflecting that in his position he probably needed to build castles in the air just to keep going.

I was brought up with a jerk, though, when he suddenly burst out: 'Marit, I'd let them amputate both my legs just to prove that I'm innocent!'

I couldn't help noticing that he had a scar high up on his chest and felt impelled to ask him what had caused it. He looked about him to make sure that no one was looking, then pulled up his shirt. My eyes must have opened wide at the sight: his whole chest

116

was a mass of scars. He then turned round and I saw
that his back was similarly scarred. The scars were
burns, probably from the fire outside his house when
he was three. Stella had mentioned the accident in
passing but she never said a word about how it had
happened.

Pee-Wee had been fetched by the guard half
an hour too late for our meeting and claimed that in
consequence he was entitled to an extra thirty minutes
to make up for it, but to no avail. At a quarter to
twelve on the dot a guard came in and said that time
was up. He wasn't even given time to say a proper
goodbye, leaving me to console myself with the
thought that I would see him again next day. Too late
I realized that I should have come at the turn of the
month, as then I would have had four consecutive
days in which to visit him, extending over two months
instead of one. That's what Korinna had done, and
now I understood why.

When we left the prison, Betty gave me a lift back to
the guesthouse. Hal had already left, as his son had
suddenly stormed off in an outburst of temper and his
father was no longer allowed to remain on the prison
premises.

'I shan't be coming here again,' Hal said,
giving me a farewell hug. He had already arranged
with Betty that she would drive me back to Hospitality
House and pick me up again next day for a second
visit to the prison. He himself planned to drive the

long way back to California the very same day. He didn't believe he would ever see his son again.

Betty was the woman I had fallen into conversation with outside the prison gates, the one who had said that my prisoner friend was very lucky. She was one of those people whom Pee-Wee with undisguised contempt had dismissed as a holy roller. I gathered that this was the derogatory term the inmates used among themselves to describe Pentecostalists and other do-gooders who tried to 'ram Christianity down their throats' in order that they might die redeemed from sin. Be that as it may, I thought Betty very nice and took to her from the start.

I also exchanged a few words with another of these self-styled missionaries. She had moved to Huntsville from England and was totally different from Betty. Every week, in the firm belief that it was God's will, she paid regular visits to some forty prisoners under sentence of death. Pee-Wee warned me that she was the biggest gossip of them all. Photographs of her in the nude were currently doing the rounds in the prison, photographs she herself had naïvely entrusted to one of the prisoners – who had promptly sold them and ensured their wider circulation.

Betty was a widow. She had moved to Huntsville from a town many miles away solely to be closer to the prison. A tall, well-built woman in her fifties, she had shoulder-length blonde hair. Heavily made-up and sporting bright red lipstick, she had an open face and a friendly smile. I met her only once or

twice during my stay but she made an indelible
impression on me, not least because of her self-
imposed calling. Without fail, every weekday, for nine
long years, she had visited the prison. She told me that
she had had many friends among the inmates who
were already dead – executed – and was continually
making new ones. For many of the prisoners she was
their sole link with the outside world.

When I got out into the open air after bidding
Pee-Wee a hurried farewell, it was to find waiting for
me a very angry Betty. I had seen her embracing
every single member of a Mexican family, from a
grandmother down to a few months' old baby, many
of them in tears.

Only on the long drive back to Hospitality
House did I discover what had upset her. The next
day, a prisoner was due to be executed and the people
I had seen Betty comforting were all members of his
family. It transpired that they had arrived at the prison
so late in the day that they would probably not be
allowed to see him for the last time.

'Had I known that, I would have visited him
myself instead of my other friend,' Betty said.
I could see that she was finding it hard to hold back
her tears.

'Tomorrow he's going to die,' she said, a catch
in her voice. 'It doesn't bear thinking about.' She then
went on to tell me how worn out she was.

'I'm not sure if I shall be able to carry on like
this for much longer,' she sighed.

That evening, as so often in the past, she intended to pray that the condemned man be granted a stay of execution. I asked her if she thought some of the men she had known who had been executed were innocent. She replied that she believed most of them really had committed the crimes of which they were accused but that she had also known a few, all of whom were by then dead, who she was convinced had been innocent. This notwithstanding, although she was irrevocably opposed to the death sentence, she couldn't help but be glad that those guilty of murder were safely behind bars.

'I'd have been terrified to meet one of them in the street,' she said.

I had occasionally found myself thinking along the same lines. What if Pee-Wee were to be granted his freedom one day? What would be my response?

***

I was utterly exhausted after four hours with Pee-Wee, but before helping myself to the guesthouse's plentiful stock of food, I decided to visit Huntsville's Texas Prison Museum.

The museum was a popular attraction and drew a stream of visitors all through the year. There was a small section containing a replica of a cell once occupied by a prisoner under sentence of death who had eventually been executed. It was very much like Pee-Wee's cell, except that he, Pee-Wee, had a table at which he could sit and write and from which he

120

could reach everything without rising from his chair.
What is more, on one wall he had been allowed to put
up all the pictures he had received from me, along
with a calendar. The cell in the museum was devoid of
all such personal items.

One showcase contained works of art
fashioned by prisoners. Most of them had been
donated to the museum after the men who made them
had been executed, though I recognized several that
were closely akin to those I had seen in Pee-Wee's
room in Hugo. I found myself wondering what the
men who had modelled and carved these delightful
wooden artefacts -- clocks, churches, animals and the
like -- had thought as they so painstakingly worked on
them.

Also on display was an old electric chair. I
shuddered at the sight, but all around me were tourists
taking it in turns to sit in it. They were all laughing
and joking, as was the guide. She said that prisoners
didn't have a wardrobe in their cell because they
didn't need one, as new clothing was issued every day.

I sat down and tried to watch a video of an
execution but the people watching with me were
talking so loudly that I was unable to follow the
commentary and was forced to give up. Instead I
began to read the notices on the walls. One read:

In 1924 the State of Texas took control of all
executions and prescribed electrocution as the
method. One of the most chilling exhibits at the
Texas Prison Museum is 'Old Sparky', the

> decommissioned electric chair in which 361
> prisoners were executed between 1924 and
> 1964. This legendary device, made by prison
> workers, was in storage at the Walls Unit Death
> House before being donated to the museum, and
> is our most controversial exhibit. In 1964
> executions were stopped while the U.S. Supreme
> Court decided on the fate of execution practices.
> Executions resumed in 1982 with lethal
> injections replacing executions as a means of
> carrying out the death penalty.[18]
> In 1964 executions were stopped while the U.S.
> Supreme Court decided on the fate of execution
> practices. Executions resumed in 1982 with
> lethal injections replacing electrocutions as a
> means of carrying out the death penalty.[18]

Not far away I was able to read about the economics involved. A judge in Florida had stated that it had now been proved that executing a prisoner cost much more than keeping him in prison for life. In the days when executions were more summary and the proceedings leading up to them less prolonged, putting people to death was much cheaper, but nowadays there are so many opportunities to appeal that the process is more complicated and expensive than simply keeping people under lock and key till the end of their days. In 1992, every execution cost Texas taxpayers more than 2.3 million dollars. That was about three times what it cost to hold a person in solitary confinement in a top-grade security prison; today it costs even more.[19]

Pee-Wee had earlier told me much the same thing:

> It is much cheaper to house a prisoner for life than to MURDER him. Another factor is the victim's family members wanting revenge. If someone killed a member of my family I'm sure I too would want that person to be held accountable for their actions. But, I wouldn't want them killed because each day they wake up and see that prison guard they will always be reminded what they are there for and know they will never be able to set another foot in a society they once knew, and his mind will torment him like a wild fire out of control. The American government has a lot of innocent blood on their hands, all in the name of the American people.

That day I went to bed at six in the evening and slept like a log till seven the next morning. Thirteen hours of uninterrupted sleep did much to help me sort out the events and impressions of the previous day and give me renewed energy.

Wednesday 13 March 1996 found me standing at the same bus stop in Huntsville where I had got off two days earlier. It was twelve hours after my second four-hour visit to Pee-Wee had come to an end. I felt that the time had passed quicker then than on the first occasion.

'Take care,' he said when we parted.
That same morning Bob told me that taking the bus to Dallas on a Wednesday might prove to be a memorable experience. When I asked him why, he merely smiled and shook his head.

Only when I stood waiting for the Greyhound did I understand what he had meant. Two days earlier I had been standing in the very same place in the dark, inwardly quaking with fear. Now, however, it was getting on for evening and there were crowds of people waiting for the same bus. Most of them, some twenty or so, ranged in age from about twenty to forty; half were white, half Afro-Americans – but they all had a small white canvas bag slung over one shoulder. My mind went back to the black-and-white gangster films that used to thrill me so when I was young. Then it dawned on me: they were newly released prisoners. I later learned that, once a week, a new batch of prisoners was released and that most of them took the bus in to Dallas.

These were the lucky ones, those who had gained their freedom after spending what may have been many years in prison. Some of them no doubt had blood on their hands. They had been returned to society with $100 each to start them off and instructions to report to their local probation officer when they reached home – assuming that they had one. Many of them could have acquired new names and new identities; I had no means of knowing. They

124

didn't appear to converse with each other very much and, as far as I could judge, they didn't know one another either; they had probably been in completely different sections of the prison.

The bus came and I joined the queue to board. To my surprise, the men waved me to the front. 'Ladies first,' one of them said gallantly.

I was lucky, as there was room for only seven more passengers, which meant that most of those waiting with me had to be left behind.

I found a seat beside a stout Afro-American woman wearing gold earrings and, although the temperature was over 20 degrees C, a blue woollen cap.

We drove out through the streets of this strange little town I had come to know so well – for good and ill.

I thought about Pee-Wee, who I might not see again for a long time to come, if ever. The last few hours we spent together had passed all too quickly. I remembered how his face had darkened when he reeled off a list of all the wrongs he believed had been done to him.

Seated just across the aisle from me was Emma. I hadn't noticed her when I boarded the bus, but now we found ourselves deep in conversation. Fifty-seven years old, she was the mother of four and had eight grandchildren. She had been to the prison to visit her son, who, like Pee-Wee, was on Death Row, and was now on her way home to Dallas after having been allowed only two hours together with him. I remember thinking that it wasn't right that someone like me, who happened to have come from a greater distance, was allowed to spend more time with prisoners than were their own family members.

Only an hour after I had bade him farewell, Pee-Wee had sat down at his typewriter to write me a letter:

> Thank you for the very loving visits, I truly enjoyed them but they went too fast and it seems like a dream. I was pissed because they didn't give me the 20 minutes they owed me. I don't know how the pictures of me turned out because as soon as they took them they escorted me back to my cell and that is where you find me now. You are probably getting back to Hospitality House now. I've had you on my mind 24 hours a day since you have left, there just wasn't enough time to absorb all of it.
>
> I know you will enjoy your stay in Atlanta with your grandson.

Enclosed with the letter was the following poem:

> *Touched by you*
> *For a moment or two*
> *you reached through*
> *my defenses too softly*
> *to caress a heart crushed*
> *askew.*

For a few magical days
you led me in tender loving ways
almost forgotten in this abyss
where caring seldom pays.
It took me a while
to see your smile
for what it really was
loving, caring and full of happiness.
I'll forever cherish you as the
days go by and give back to you
today, that very same loving SMILE.

ELLIS UNIT'S DOS AND DON'TS

Some three or four weeks after my visit to Huntsville, I had a letter from the Texas Department of Criminal Justice. I didn't recognize the handwriting on the envelope and my name was wrongly spelt. I couldn't help but feel a stab of fear at the sight. Had something serious happened to Pee-Wee? Was he already dead?

I was relieved to find that it only was a pink form to say that I had broken one of the prison rules. I had sent an inmate a photograph of himself, and that was not allowed.

My 'crime', such as it was, was that, after I had said goodbye to Pee-Wee and just before leaving, one of the guards had taken pictures of him for me with a Polaroid camera. I had paid for this when I checked in that day; the photographs had cost $3 each. The guard had taken four in all, two for Pee-Wee and two for me, but unfortunately they all turned out to be very poor. For that reason I had had mine enlarged and sent one of them to Pee-Wee, along with a covering letter. This, it appeared, was against the rules, as the photograph was classed as 'contraband'. I never found out whether the letter was similarly withheld from Pee-Wee, but from the pink form I did discover a whole lot of things that were not allowed. It was enough if:

The letter contains threats of physical harm against any person or place or threats of criminal activity.

The letter threatens blackmail or extortion.

The letter concerns sending contraband in or out of the institution.

The letter concerns plans to escape or unauthorized entry.

The letter concerns plans for activities and violation of institutional rules.

The letter concerns plans for future criminal activities.

The letter is in code and its contents are not understood by the reader.

The letter solicits gifts of goods or money under false pretenses or for payment to other inmates.

The letter contains a graphic presentation of sexual behavior that is in violation of the law.

The letter contains information which, if communicated, would create a clear and present danger of violence or physical harm to a human being.

The photograph, and possibly the letter as well, had been confiscated because it concerned 'plans for future criminal activities'. It seems ridiculous, but it still irks me to think that I could be accused of such a thing.

Something similar had happened two years earlier, when I sent Pee-Wee drawing paper and envelopes to save him money. The authorities sent me a similar form then too, and Pee-Wee had patiently explained to me that this was not permitted and that we just had to accept it. It was the same when I faxed him via the prison's administrative authorities; they politely but firmly informed me that that was strictly forbidden.

I wasn't even allowed to send him postage stamps. I knew Pee-Wee liked attractive foreign stamps, so I had often taken pains to put pictorials on the letters I sent him. After taking so much trouble, I was disappointed to learn that the prison authorities tested and marked all stamps with a special felt pen to check for drugs.

Pee-Wee had told me that once, when I had sent him a stamp commemorating the art of printing, for some reason it had not been thus defaced. Whether this was an oversight or someone in the Postal Department had thought it a shame to spoil such a beautiful picture, I shall never know.

Whatever the reason, Pee-Wee was resigned to the strictness of the prison rules. He said that the Postal Department had to cope with some 20,000 letters daily, so it was understandable that a careful check had to be kept on them.

The only things prisoners were allowed to receive were books from an approved bookshop – provided they came direct. This notwithstanding, when I asked my publisher to send Pee-Wee a copy of my latest children's book, complete with an official stamp and the name and address of the company, he never got it. I tried twice, but each time the book was returned.

One day I received another handwritten letter from
Pee-Wee. He had run out of ribbons for the typewriter
his parents had bought him, and he didn't have any
stamps left either. I decided to send him a hundred
dollars. I'd been doing this for some time, twice a year,
to enable him to buy drawing materials, notepaper
and stamps.

It was a complicated procedure. First, I had to
write out a cheque drawn on a Norwegian bank,
which then sent it by post to a specified address, from
where it was credited to Pee-Wee's account in the
prison. I had to complete a form, too, which was
enclosed with the cheque. It was a laborious process,
but it worked and Pee-Wee always received the
money.

Prisoners were at liberty to buy small items on
sale inside the prison. In the first letter I received from
Amnesty, they pointed out that most prisoners were
virtually penniless. That was true of Pee-Wee, too, but
to his credit he never directly asked me for money; on
the other hand, he made no attempt to conceal the
fact that he was strapped for cash.

Some months after I received the letter from the
prison chiding me for having sent him 'contraband', I
had another letter from Pee-Wee. I had told him
earlier that I would like to write to his sisters and urge
them to visit him. In reply he thanked me for trying to
help, but said he thought it would be a waste of time.
He had given up all hope of having either of them

come to see him. In all the years he had spent on Death Row, never once had they paid him a visit, despite their living less than a day's drive away. The only person to have visited him was his mother, but when he wrote, it had been over a year since she had last been there.

I had recently had a letter from Stella in which she did her best to explain why Pee-Wee's sisters never went to see him. The engine of Jane's car had burnt out and Grace had just had another baby and, as if that were not enough, was working practically every evening.

I had no difficulty in understanding the problem. Had Pee-Wee been my own brother, I know I would never have felt able to visit him either. And had he been my son, the whole situation would have been unbearable. I felt immensely sorry for Stella, who had worked so hard to help her errant son. She was growing sicker with every day that passed, smoking more and more cigarettes and having serious trouble with her breathing. I couldn't help but wonder how long she had to live.

***

> I'm not afraid of dying. I pity those who are going to kill me. Those are the ones suffering, not me. It is the American state I blame. I am another person now than the one I once was, and I will be this other person when I get out. I will never do the same mistakes. I know this.

I could tell from Pee-Wee's letter that he was finding
things difficult. He had still not had a decision on his
latest appeal and was afraid it would be turned down.
I knew that he was doing all he could to find
something in the law that would impel the authorities
to review his case once again, and recalled what Hal
had said about relatives tending to lose hope before
the prisoners, who never gave up hoping.

The denial came three months later, towards
the end of February 1996. From the papers Stella sent
me, I learned that one of the judges at the Texas
Court of Criminal Justice had dissented. Before a
decision was reached, this judge, Charlie Baird, had
told the presiding judge that he thought Pee-Wee
should be granted a new hearing. In his opinion, the
court had not properly fulfilled its duties.[20]

Personally, I very much wanted to believe Pee-
Wee. I couldn't understand how he could strive so
hard to prove his innocence if he was actually guilty.
Only a short time previously he had written to me:

> There is nothing that connects me to that
> murder. I wasn't there. You have to believe
> me!

His protestations notwithstanding, I was still in doubt.
What about the bowl of ice cream with his fingerprints
on it? Wasn't that proof enough? Both yes and no:
Pee-Wee maintained that his prints must have come
from an earlier visit.

Over and over again I pondered what could have happened in Lula Mae Denning's house. My mind was full of questions to which I had no answers. Was Pee-Wee telling the truth or was he lying? Or had he simply suppressed all memory of what had occurred that fateful afternoon? He had once told me that it was impossible for him to have suppressed the memory of something so horrendous – and he seemed absolutely sincere. Could he have become embroiled in a lie of his own making, a figment of his imagination? Was he himself firmly convinced that what he said was true?

For me personally it was of no great importance whether Pee-Wee was guilty or not guilty. As I saw it, my principal task was to prove to him that I was his friend and that I believed him, though deep in my heart I had my doubts, as did those who were close to him.

'Do you believe me?' was the first thing he had asked every new lawyer assigned to him.

If they appeared reluctant to answer, he had immediately sent them packing, and I was afraid the same thing might happen to me. That is why I never breathed a word of my doubts. But I never said that I believed him, either – which may explain why he was so eager to convince me of his innocence.

I sat down to write my thirty-fourth letter to him, a letter in which I reiterated that I very much wanted to believe him and that I hoped his appeal would prove successful.

I finished the letter, sealed the envelope and dropped it into the nearest mailbox.

That same year, 1996, 45 prisoners were executed in the United States, but 'only' three in Texas.[21]

HELPING HANDS

Korinna and I did our best to support each other. We were both worried about what would happen to Pee-Wee, but there was little we could do, other than try to brighten his lonely existence.

A year after I had first visited him, I got to know Ward Larkin. Ward was in his early forties and lived in Houston, where he was a member of the Texas Coalition to Abolish the Death Penalty (TCADP), a branch of the National Coalition to Abolish the Death Penalty (NCADP). He was a regular visitor to Huntsville, where he went to see prisoners under sentence of death.

I asked him if he would consider visiting Pee-Wee.

In April 1997 I wrote to Pee-Wee to tell him that Ward would be happy to visit him if he, Pee-Wee, would put him on his visitors list. I also told him that I had found Ward's name on the Internet and that all I knew about him was that he worked for an organization dedicated to abolition of the death penalty. I said that he was an active member of the organization and that there was a lot about him on the net and that he sounded very professional and capable.

I was careful to emphasize that the decision was his, Pee-Wee's, and his alone, and that it was solely up to him to decide if he would like a visit from time to time. The only thing I told Ward about Pee-Wee was that he was an interesting and intelligent man with next to no visitors.

I concluded my letter by warning Pee-Wee that he was to look upon Ward as a friend and treat him as such. I knew from experience that he reacted strongly to people and that there were some he disliked from the start.

I need not have worried. Pee-Wee responded immediately by putting Ward on his visitors list and wishing him welcome.

In an email Ward sent me after his first visit, he said that Pee-Wee – whom he always referred to by his real name, Ivan – had been very intense but that he thought that quite understandable in the circumstances, as meeting someone for the first time can be a trying experience under normal circumstances, and Pee-Wee's circumstances were anything but normal. He also said that he regretted not having visited Pee-Wee first on the day he went to Huntsville.

He had promised Pee-Wee that he would see him again the next time he visited the prison, which would be in some four to six weeks' time. He said he was touched by the fact that, following his first visit, Pee-Wee had sent him a thank-you letter, but that he found it distressing to have had to say goodbye to four prisoners who were due to be executed within the next six weeks. He even listed their names: Clifford Belyeu, Bruce Callins, Dorsie Johnson and Ireneo Tristan

Montoya. He knew Montoya's parents, who were also visiting at the time, and had chanced on two more women he knew, one visiting her husband, the other her son. I couldn't help but reflect on what Ward had dedicated his life to doing and the reason. He wasn't religious, so that could be ruled out. However, fifteen years earlier he had worked in the Middle East, where he had seen executions, most of them beheadings, with his own eyes. He had returned home strongly opposed to the death penalty but did nothing to combat it until he was introduced to the TCADP. From then onwards he had done little else but work to save men and women on Death Row.

This was at a time when emailing was rapidly gaining strength, which made communication between Ward and myself much simpler than that between Pee-Wee and me, which was confined to ordinary mail. I wrote and thanked Ward for his willingness to pay regular visits to Pee-Wee and expressed my admiration for what he was doing. In reply he told me that it wasn't the visits in themselves that were difficult but that what worried him was that some of the prisoners had begun to think that he could get them a reprieve. He had made it clear that he wasn't a lawyer but that he would do what he could, and that sometimes his offer was misunderstood and a prisoner would come to believe that he was doing his best to have his sentence commuted. He added that he was glad that Pee-Wee realized that he could do nothing to help him in that way. The TCADP didn't deal with specific cases: their aim was to bring about

abolition of the death penalty per se, not to obtain
reprieves for prisoners.

I found it comforting to learn that Ward, like
myself and many other people, felt that he could not
fail prisoners whom he already knew.

1 June 1997

> I did receive a visit from Ward and he is a
> very nice person. I had a great visit from him,
> plus he sent me a law book and some
> stationery which helped me out a lot. I have
> only said to him about you, that you are a very
> nice lady and that you have helped me out a
> lot. I will not talk to him or anyone else about
> our relationship because that is between us
> only. I'm not sure about what you will think
> about 'Texas Coalition to Abolish the Death
> Penalty' because most of them are very anti-
> Government and I don't agree with everything
> they do or say, they speak more out for the
> blacks and Hispanics than they do for any
> other race and I don't agree with any of that at
> all, Texas has executed more white people
> than any other, plus there is more white
> people on death row than any other race.

I had heard Pee-Wee express similar opinions before,
and when I visited his family in Oklahoma, I had seen
how proud they were to be of Native Indian stock.
Pee-Wee had some of this pride himself, though he

saw himself primarily as an ordinary white American.
He sincerely believed that blacks were treated better
than whites and that he would have received more
help from a wide range of organizations had he been
black. I found that hard to credit, but he insisted that
that was the way it was.

A little later, also in June, I received an email
from Ward:

> The times that I visit Ivan are going well.
> There were a couple of times that he started to
> talk about how he doesn't like blacks, nor
> Jews. And I'm sure he noticed by the look on
> my face that I wasn't going to agree with him,
> so he quickly changed the subject. Otherwise
> we tend to agree with socio-political-economic
> ideologies.
> It is very difficult to be in Texas right now.
> Twenty men have been executed already this
> year. I think it was eight in the month of May.
> There have already been four in the month of
> June. And there is a man scheduled to be
> executed tomorrow.
> I have met a couple of foreign journalist teams
> just this week. There is a documentary film
> crew from Berlin Germany doing a film that
> involves a death row inmate. Also I am
> meeting an Italian News crew at the airport in
> 1:30 hours.

I was glad that I had been able to bring Ward and
Pee-Wee together and hoped that their meeting

would help to alleviate Pee-Wee's loneliness. But was
he lonely? He had never said anything to that effect.

Towards the end of the month, Pee-Wee wrote again:

> The weather is changing here, it has been very
> nice. I played a few games of baseball. I would
> like to be fishing right now, it is the best time
> to go, especially after all the rain we had last
> week, it rained for three days.
> None of us know when – or how – we will
> leave this world, but we know that someday
> we will and that is why it is so important to
> choose the people in our lives today while we
> can be happy, because we never know if we
> will live to see another day.
> I wish I could be out in the nature right now
> because I know it is the most beautiful of the
> season, everything is turning green and
> different colors. Plus, I love to go fishing and
> this is the best time to go, this is the time when
> the big fish are biting. I hope someday soon
> I will be able to go.
> I have a higher power that helps me get
> through my days and it helps me maintain my
> composure.

Pee-Wee was always waiting for something, either that
his appeal would be upheld, that he would be believed
and be granted a new hearing, or that the date set for
his execution would be postponed. That's how it was
on Death Row.

In the summer of 1997, yet another of Pee-Wee's appeals was denied:

> I just found out that the Federal court turned down my writ. I have two more steps to go, but if I do not get a hearing granted, the state will kill me. I can't get the help I need for an investigator and the court won't appoint me one, so I will probably die next year.

I couldn't help but think that he was being subjected to slow torture.

In August 1997 Pee-Wee sent me the latest news about his father, whom he had neither seen nor spoken to since he was sent to prison:

> I have gotten so much bad news the last month that I have just taken the time to reflect on what has been happening in my life. I will tell you all the news, starting with my father. They thought at the hospital that he had a heart attack, once they'd done tests on him they found tumors and black spots on his lungs and the tumors were malignant, he has advanced lung cancer. It really bothers me because I can't be there with him.

A few days later he wrote to say that he had learned from one of his mother's friends that she had given up smoking, probably on account of her husband's lung cancer. Pee-Wee knew that his father was undergoing radiation therapy, but he had heard nothing from his mother for a long time. He hadn't heard anything from other members of his family either, much to his disappointment. They were always promising to visit him, he said, but something always seemed to turn up to prevent it. He hadn't heard a word from his father all the time he had been on Death Row and his father hadn't even attended his trial – according to Stella, because he just couldn't stand the strain involved. One day, however, Pee-Wee wrote happily to say:

> I got to talk for 20 minutes on the phone with my father. He was home alone.

I was very glad to learn that, at long last, the two were talking together again.

All this time, Pee-Wee had continued his unrelenting efforts to obtain help from sources outside the prison -- from his former teachers, the Church and the few friends he still had left. Towards the end of August he wrote:

> You know, it is getting real bad here, the state executed 6 people in April and there are 9 people with dates for next month. The Attorney General said he has the vision of at least 80 executions this year. You know the Americans can point their fingers at other countries because of their Human Rights record, but they are murdering their own citizens. They are always on Chinas back because of their Human Rights record.

The District Attorney never realized his dream to the full, but he came close, as that year, 1997, 74 people were executed in the United States, 37 of them in Texas.[22]

In February 1998 Ward emailed me to say that he had visited Pee-Wee, who had been ill with influenza for over a month. He said there had only been five visitors to the prison while he was there, as the attention of people in the town was centred on something quite different. That day, 3 February, Karla Faye Tucker was executed in the prison; she was the first woman to be executed in the US since 1984 and the first in Texas since 1863.[23] In consequence, journalists had flooded in from all over the world, Norway included, Ward said. As the time for Tucker's execution, six o'clock in the evening, drew nearer, some 200 reporters and 1,000 or more ordinary citizens gathered outside The Walls. I had read a lot about Tucker myself, including the fact that she had married the prison chaplain and, in the course of the fourteen years she spent on Death Row, had undergone a complete change of personality. This notwithstanding, every attempt to have her reprieved was turned down by the Governor, George W. Bush. Ward also informed me that Stella had not been to visit Pee-Wee as she had promised and that he and Pee-Wee had discussed Socrates and Plato. Pee-Wee had told him that his father's health had improved following his radiation treatment.

144

But his father must have been much sicker than anyone realized, as, only three months later, Ward wrote to say that he was dead. I immediately sent Pee-Wee my condolences.

He took his father's death extremely badly. He was both saddened and angry at not being allowed to attend the funeral. In protest, he shaved his head and announced that he intended to continue to do so for the rest of his life in honour of his father, who, because of the radiation, had likewise lost his hair.

> My father died on May 7 1998 at 5 am. I shaved my head because my father lost all his hair to the chemotherapy treatments that he had and I want to show my father that I love him by shaving all my hair off.

To his bitter disappointment, not even then did any of his family come to visit him. On 1 July he wrote me to say that if none of them had been to see him by the end of the month, he would take them off his visitors list and have no more to do with them.

For a long time after his father's death, I could tell that Pee-Wee was deeply depressed. After a while, however, things began to pick up and he even got himself a small job, that of cutting his fellow prisoners' hair for a couple of hours each day. This allowed him to visit some of the other men on Death Row, which he thoroughly enjoyed, as it enabled him to chat freely with other 'old-timers'. I wrote back to say that he must have gained the prison authorities' confidence if he was allowed the use of razors and scissors.

His pleasure proved short-lived, however, as Ward told me that he had been punished for some misdemeanor or other. I asked Pee-Wee what had happened and it transpired that he had been caught in possession of cigarettes that he was planning to sell. This had earned him a spell of solitary confinement and loss of privileges.

> Well, I am not perfect, that is for sure. My cell was searched and the guard found 130 cigarettes and that is what got me put in solitary. I spent 52 days in that sweat box, 15 days without my fan and property. I have it all back except for my craft supplies, I have six months of piddling restriction.

Although he had threatened to do so, in the event Pee-Wee never took his family members off his visitors list. Not only that, one day he told me that his mother had been to see him:

> When the guards came to get me, they said I had a special visitor and I couldn't think of who it was, so when I saw my mother sitting there, I was happy.

It came as no great surprise to me to learn from his next letter that neither his brother nor either of his two sisters had turned up. I don't think he was overly surprised.

146

With limited opportunities of lodging further appeals, Pee-Wee concentrated his efforts on saving his life. He wrote letter after letter to lawyers and government officials and his letters to me were full of news about how his case was going.

I later learned from official sources that in 1998, no fewer than 68 people were executed in the United States, 20 of them in Texas.[24]

LAST MEETING

Three years after my first meeting with Pee-Wee, I was afforded a chance to visit him again, which prompted me to write to Stella to ask if she would consider joining me in Huntsville. She had told Pee-Wee that she intended to visit him.

The fact is that I was planning to attend (in March 1999) a four-week Spanish course for Norwegian journalists in the small town of Antigua in Guatemala, where there were numerous language schools, so it would be easy for me to fit this in with a visit to Huntsville on my way home.

When I landed in Houston, I was full of new impressions after my month in Guatemala, where it had been spring. Now I was looking forward to enjoying a second spring in the US.

Ward met me at the airport. He had invited me to stay with him and his parents over the weekend before the two of us went on to Huntsville. I should mention that I had met him once before, briefly one morning, when he came to Norway for a winter holiday.

I had no difficulty in picking him out at the airport, as he towered head and shoulders above the rest of the people waiting. In the meantime he had grown a beard, long and grizzled. He asked me if

I thought he looked like Henrik Ibsen. Not sure what to say, I replied that he did, a little, but refrained from pointing out that Norway's literary giant had actually been quite short.

Ward loaded his little car with my suitcases, which were full of presents for people back home, then drove me at a leisurely speed to meet his parents. They proved to be a nice, homely couple living in what, by American (though not Norwegian) standards, was a small but roomy house in the suburbs. I was given a pleasant little room of my own with a lovely big bed. It was wonderful to shower once again in steaming hot water after four weeks of nothing but cold water in Guatemala.

I learned that five times a year people like me came from all over the world to stay with Ward and his parents, whose home served as a halfway house en route to the prison. Joan, Ward's mother, told me she enjoyed having people from abroad staying with them and that, because of their son's dedication to the cause, they too were opposed to the death penalty.

Ward told me that he was currently visiting seven men under sentence of death in addition to Pee-Wee. Every third week he would regularly spend a morning in Huntsville, which was no more than an hour and a half's drive from Houston. Each time he would visit two prisoners, spending two hours with each of them. He told me that he had many times said a final farewell to a prisoner, on several occasions just a day or two before the man concerned was executed. He had attended only one execution, and that was because the prisoner had himself requested that he do so.

Ward was a man of few words, but he confided in me that for a long time afterwards he hadn't been himself. He said that when the man involved, who had become a good friend, had been given the lethal injection, he had felt as if his own soul had left his body and was floating above him, just beneath the ceiling.

His words surprised me. To me, he appeared to be a very down-to-earth sort of person and I had never suspected that he harboured such thoughts.

I asked him if he was likely to attend another execution but all he would say was that he didn't know. For my part, I sincerely hoped that Pee-Wee would never ask me.

After I got to know Ward, it became easier for me to send Pee-Wee messages of a more personal nature. Whenever he was planning to visit Huntsville, Ward would email me to ask if there was anything I'd like him to pass on to Pee-Wee that I couldn't write about. My mind went back to stories I had read of censorship when Norway was occupied during the Second World War. But this was present-day, peacetime America. The important thing was, though, that now Pee-Wee could have someone visit him every four or five weeks.

That same evening, Ward took me on a tour of downtown Houston. We parked outside the courthouse, where countless judgments had been handed down over the years, and in the gathering dusk walked round the vast bulk of the Federal Detention Center, which housed close on a thousand prisoners. We walked and walked in the cold and wet until I began to wonder if we would ever reach wherever we were heading. Ward pointed out objects of interest and regaled me with tales of police misconduct and other dramatic incidents linked to crime in America. He said that only a few years earlier there had been a case involving a psychotic woman who, fearing that she was about to have an attack, phoned for an ambulance to take her to a psychiatric clinic. As a precaution, in such cases the police are also alerted, but by mischance they arrived before the ambulance. Thinking they had come to take her into custody, when they rang the bell the woman panicked and grabbed a breadknife to defend herself with. When she refused to let them in, they broke down the door and, as she was still holding the knife, shot her repeatedly in the chest. Ward recounted this and other such happenings quite calmly, as though they were everyday occurrences. Not for the first time, I could only wonder how such things could happen in this day and age.

Ward seemed to have a new story to tell at every street corner, so much so that I began to feel rather uncomfortable and wonder what I was doing there. The thought struck me that I didn't know him all that well and that, apart from us, there wasn't a soul about.

We eventually came to a busier and better-lit street, where we found ourselves a place on the terrace of a nearby restaurant. Ward ordered a beer for himself and a glass of wine for me. We were surrounded by people, all of them laughing and talking. It turned out that this was the theatre district and that, knowing I edited a magazine devoted to the theatre, he had chosen the restaurant with that in mind. The next day was a Sunday and he had booked tickets for us at a theatre close to his parents' house.

As I have said, Ward was a man of few words – except when it was a matter of the death penalty, for which reason I often tried to steer the conversation in that direction. This usually resulted in ever more stories and a flow of useful information. As it was a Saturday, the prison was closed to visitors, which did not admit outsiders at weekends. I couldn't help but reflect on how inconvenient that must have been for people bound to a normal working week.

***

On the Monday – this was towards the end of March 1999 – the two of us set off for Huntsville. Ward insisted that I should drive, to get used to the car. He had generously offered me use of it for a couple of days following our visit to the prison. He himself planned to take a Greyhound bus back to Houston later that same day.

It was just coming on to spring. The leaves of the trees were a fresh pale green and the grassy verges of the motorway were carpeted with lovely mauve flowers. I remarked on the frequency of road signs and Ward told me that I risked being arrested if I continued to drive as slowly as I was doing. Needless to say, from then on I put my foot down and kept it down!

We made straight for Ellis Unit. We had agreed that I should visit Pee-Wee alone, as Ward was intending to see two other prisoners. He warned me that things had been tightened up considerably since my first visit three years earlier, the reason being that, just before Christmas, an inmate under sentence of death had somehow managed to escape and that the remaining prisoners had been punished en bloc in consequence. All the men held in Ellis Unit had been deprived of rights they had earned by good conduct, for example, and for a long time were not even allowed visitors. Letters were confiscated and they were not permitted to buy personal items from the prison store. This was a severe blow to Pee-Wee, as it meant that he was no longer able to purchase pencils, crayons and drawing paper.

I found it hard to understand how anyone could escape from such a heavily guarded prison. I was told that no one had escaped from Ellis Unit since the breakout by a member of the legendary Bonnie and Clyde gang more than sixty years earlier.

In the event, freedom for the escaper, Martin Gurule, proved short-lived, as he was found dead not far from the prison ten days later. Rumour had it that it was an accident: his bloated body was found in a river, where he had either frozen to death or drowned. There's no telling what his life would have been like in the prison had he been recaptured, as all his fellow-prisoners were furious with him because they had been made to suffer as a result of his action.

We took off at a turning near the prison, where there was a guardhouse.

'We're only a few hundred yards from the entrance now,' Ward said. 'You'll need to show your passport and state the prisoner's name and ID number. They'll check the whole car, so you'll have to open the trunk, too.'

At that moment the heavens opened! The rain simply poured down. Ward remained sitting in the car, leaving the formalities to me, as he knew that I would have to go through the same procedure alone the following day. The stony-faced, grey-uniformed guard had difficulty getting my name right on his notepad, which was soaking wet, and couldn't even determine my nationality; in the end I had to help him by saying that I was Norwegian.

Once past this preliminary hurdle, I drove on for a further hundred yards or so and parked the car.

As on my first visit three years earlier, I had to leave my handbag and camera in the car.

That apart, the procedure had changed since I was last there. No longer were our passports hauled up into one of the watchtowers. Instead, one at a time, we were subjected to a body search. I was asked if I had

154

brought anything with me and answered that all I had was a lipstick.

'You can't take that in with you,' the guard said.

That was a blow. I didn't know what to do. I could have given it to her or simply thrown it into a waste bin, but it was new and had cost quite a lot. In the end I was allowed to go back to the car and leave it there. I was so het up that I actually ran both there and back! My nerves were already on edge and that did nothing to help. While all this was happening, Ward just stayed put, chuckling to himself at my plight.

We were then sluiced into the prison itself. On our way into the Visitors Room I again had to pass the little hatch where we had to hand in our passports and entry permits. Here one could order photographs of the prisoner one was visiting.

'I'm sorry,' the woman on duty said, 'but we're out of film.'

'If I buy a film in town and bring it along tomorrow, will you take photos for me?' I asked.

The woman promised to make enquiries and let me know if that would be in order.

I was allotted seat no. 13. We entered the Visitors Room and, as on the first occasion, I sat down to wait − − and wait -- and wait. Ward was seated on the opposite side of the horseshoe, where Hal had sat on my first visit. Then the prisoners were brought in, one at a time.

Pee-Wee had still not come. I fell into conversation with some of the others who were waiting, most of them women, as had been the case the last time I was there. Some of the 'missionaries' were present, too. My attention was caught by a good-looking woman whom I later learned was English and named Hester. She was married to the prisoner she was visiting. They had probably started off as pen-friends, as had I. The two of us got up to buy snacks and something to drink, the only things we were allowed to give to prisoners, only to find that all the vending machines were practically empty, as they had not been replenished over the weekend. Hester was furious.

'It's sickening!' she fumed.

When I returned to my seat, it was to find that Pee-Wee had still not come. I'd been perched on that hard wooden chair for almost an hour. At that moment one of the guards came over to me.

'I've enquired about that film,' he said brusquely. 'There'll be no film here tomorrow either, and you're not allowed to bring your own.'

At long last Pee-Wee was brought in, right at the tail-end of the line of prisoners.

The first thing that caught my eye was his body. He'd put on a lot of weight in the three years since I'd last seen him, and his breathing was noticeably laboured. My mind immediately went back to Stella: he'd grown so like her. He was still handcuffed, but the cuffs were removed once he was safely inside the 'cage within a cage'. His head was shaved, as he had told me it would be, and without his dark curly locks he seemed even more overweight.

Only when he was firmly settled in his seat behind the glass that separated us did I see the greatest change in him: all life had left his eyes, leaving them dull and listless. He looked resigned, which I found surprising, as there had been no hint of any such thing in his letters.

The first hours in his presence dragged immeasurably. Nine years on Death Row had taken their toll, although I had the feeling that he had still not given up entirely.

Pee-Wee was, after all, still alive and still fighting, and, as always, his conversation was mostly about his case and the injustice of his sentence and his struggle to regain his freedom. Eighteen months had elapsed since September 1997, when he had lodged another appeal – the outcome of which he still did not know -- after having found what he perceived as an error in the record of the court proceedings.

On my first visit he had told me that if ever he were released, he would study medicine. Now he said the same.

I told him about my four weeks in Guatemala, and he perked up when I described the fun we had had with our Spanish teacher, how I had danced salsa every week and how colourful I had found the Maya Indians. He actually smiled when I told him about the family I had stayed with, the cold showers I'd taken every morning, the simple meals and the trip on potholed roads to Honduras.

All the time he sat rocking to and fro in his chair, ears
cocked. It was nice to have someone listening to what
I had to say for a change and not to be interrupted
every few minutes with talk of other things.

When I had finished my account, Pee-Wee
went on to tell me about his own life. He still
meditated for two hours each day and practised
siddha yoga. He was firmly convinced that a better life
awaited him after this one and he assured me once
again that he was not afraid of dying. He seemed
wholly sincere when he said that, and I felt that he
was. I noticed that he shrugged his shoulders
resignedly more than he had the first time we met but
was smiling more.

All in all, we spent some rewarding hours in
each other's company and he seemed to appreciate
my having come to see him again. He spoke more or
less without pause and several times asked me if I
understood what he was saying. He knew I was in
touch with his mother but didn't want her to know
how disappointed he was that none of his family had
been to visit him in prison. He was determined to be
positive and made it clear that there was no point in
bemoaning his fate. Then, in an aside, he remarked,
quite casually: 'They're executing a man tomorrow,
by the way.'

He gestured towards the far side of the room,
where what looked to me to be an old man, but who I
later learned was only in his sixties, was sitting. I had
noticed him earlier, as there had been a lot of coming
and going where he sat, which was highly unusual. I

158

later learned that on the last day before a prisoner was due to be executed, there was no limit on the number of visitors he was allowed to have.

Pee-Wee told me something about him. His name was Robert Excell White and he was known far and wide as the person who had spent the longest time on Death Row in an American prison -- twenty-five years. Born in 1938, he had been in prison since 1974.[25] Because of this, press coverage was expected to be formidable – as, indeed, it proved to be.

Every so often I would cast a glance around the room and see White and his visitors laughing and joking together. I realized that they were doing all they could to keep each other's spirits up. Pee-Wee told me what lay ahead for White, or Excell as he was known in the prison. At eleven next morning he would be taken over to The Walls, where, later in the day, he would be served his last meal, a meal of his own choosing. Then, sometime before six in the evening, he would be strapped down on a gurney.

'By law, a person condemned to death must be executed on a weekday before six in the evening,' Pee-Wee told me. He explained that the law had come into force in 1995 to set a time most convenient to the prisoner's dependents. Previously, prisoners had been executed at midnight to ensure that a possible last-minute reprieve reached the prison in time. Midnight was still the rule in a number of states.

'There, on the gurney, he is given his first injection, an innocuous saline solution, and then a couple of lethal ones and that's it,' Pee-Wee said laconically. He gave me a searching look to see how I reacted.

I resolved to go over to The Walls the following day and join the Amnesty demonstration to be held there.

In the course of this second visit to Pee-Wee I discovered that he had friends in the prison, though he'd never said anything to that effect in his letters to me. One of them was Michael, whom Ward regularly visited. I learned that Michael was the man seated next to Pee-Wee in the Visitors Room. It was then that, to my surprise, Ward, after having first visited another prisoner, came over and took the seat next to me.

It turned out that it was Pee-Wee who had prevailed on Ward to visit Michael too, as no one else ever came to see him. The two greeted each other through the glass. Michael was a good-looking young man with clear blue eyes.

'He's little more than a child, as you can see,' Pee-Wee said. He had clearly taken him under his wing.

When I rose to leave, Michael uttered four short words that went straight to my heart: 'Stay out of trouble.'

He, better than most, knew just what that implied. He had spent only two years or so behind bars, but was doomed to languish on Death Row for many more suspenseful months and years without knowing what fate held in store for him.[26] In the

160

event, following the 1995 Oklahoma City bomb
outrage, Texas amended the law to reduce the time
allowed for appeals,[27] with the consequence that
Michael was executed ahead of many of his fellow
prisoners.[28]

On the drive back to Huntsville Ward told me that
Michael hated blacks and that he had often been
criticized for visiting him. He invariably countered his
critics by saying:

'If I can accept a person who has committed
murder, I can also accept that that person is a racist.'
That, he said, was usually enough to silence any
criticism.

To make his point, Ward had warned racist
prisoners, Michael among them, that if they continued
to talk that way, he would stop visiting them. Over
the years, he may well have helped to change the
attitudes of many Ellis Unit inmates.

I dropped Ward off at the bus station, where
he was to take the Greyhound bus back to Houston. It
was the same one as I had found myself standing in,
tremulous and alone, three years earlier. As I have
said, the plan was that I would hand the car back a
day or so later, before returning to Norway via
Atlanta.

First, however, I had four more brief hours
ahead of me together with Pee-Wee. I resolved to
listen more intently to what he had to say and talk less
myself; I reasoned that I could always say what I
wanted to in my letters.

This time too I stayed at Hospitality House. As it happened, Bob, the manager, was away on a week's vacation, together with his wife, and the establishment was being run by another couple, Jacky and Charles. They too were Baptists, and all they did was done in God's name. Jacky talked incessantly. To be honest, I wasn't sure that I liked them. I had barely spoken to them before, as Ward and I had driven straight on to the prison the morning we arrived. I consoled myself with the thought that the first time I had stayed there, I had thoroughly enjoyed it, so I hoped to do so again.

However, now the whole house had an overhanging air of gloom, though I was unable to ascertain the cause.

Then the doorbell rang. The newcomers proved to be members of Robert White's family. I got talking to White's sister, who told me that she hadn't seen her brother for fourteen years and that she had come to Huntsville to witness his execution, which was scheduled to take place within the next twenty-four hours. Now there was to be a prayer meeting at Hospitality House.

The ceremony was presided over by Jacky and Charles, and they invited me to join in. We stood in a circle in the day room while a short prayer was said for the condemned man's soul. I realized that this was a routine occurrence, but I couldn't help thinking how strange it was to be standing there, holding hands with a woman whose brother was about to die.

The family only stayed for a quarter of an hour or so, and when they had left Jacky and Charles

invited me to share their chicken dinner. We ate
straight from the paper the chicken was wrapped in.

When we had finished our meal and they had
thanked God for what we had eaten, Charles sat down
and set about cutting strip cartoons out of newspapers
and pasting them into small notebooks.

Suddenly, without looking up from his task, he
asked me what kind of grass we had in our garden in
Norway.

Taken aback by the unexpected question, I
could only reply that I had no idea. I couldn't help
wondering, though, how he could talk about
something so trivial when a man was scheduled to be
put to death only a few hours later, a bare stone's
throw from where we were sitting.

Unable to contain myself, when I had
recovered my composure, I told him how abhorrent I
found it that Robert White was to be killed by the
state.

'We don't kill them, they're executed,' he said
matter-of-factly, without pausing in what he was
doing. 'Anyway, it's only right and proper that White
should be executed,' he added. 'He's been on Death
Row for far too long.'

My eyes fell on a text on the wall:

God so loved the world
Prayer changes things
Christ is a new creation
Don't count sheep
Talk to the shepherd

Also on the wall was a framed picture beneath which, spelled out in toothpicks, were the words:

Dedicated to the glory of God

Only then did I realize why I felt so oppressed by the all-pervading gloom. It wasn't that I was opposed to Christianity as such but more the general acceptance that all that happened was in accordance with God's will.

That it was God's will that the prisoners languishing on Death Row should die – and that they deserved to. A moment ago, Jacky and Charles had been standing with tears in their eyes, praying for a man awaiting imminent death, hand in hand with members of his family, and now here they were, trying to convince me that it was right that he should die. I found it hard to contain my anger. These people were wholly devoid of political opinions; to them, everything was God's will.

I had no choice but to remain in the guesthouse for the rest of the evening. None of the people who had been with me in the Visitors Room were staying there; I was the only guest. I resolved to phone Pee-Wee's younger brother, to ask him if Stella was coming to see Pee-Wee while I was there. She and I had agreed to meet but I hadn't heard a word from her since. He told me that his mother was out playing bingo and that he didn't think she would be coming to Huntsville. I knew it was difficult for the family to relate to Pee-Wee, but this was too much.

'Don't you realize,' I said, 'that Pee-Wee feels that none of you care about him any longer? I think it's time some of you changed your attitudes and came to see him. He feels badly let down and deserted by his family. He doesn't want you to know about it, but I know how disheartened he is. I can see it in his eyes — the light's gone out of them.'

'But we haven't let him down,' was the reply. 'Of course we care about him.'

There was a long silence.

'What do you want me to say to him tomorrow, then?' I asked.

'Tell him we'll write. Tell him we love him.'

That was a crumb of comfort if nothing else, but I doubted very much if any of them would ever make good on that promise and actually put pen to paper.

Some days in my life are blanks, completely erased from my memory. The day of my second visit to Pee-Wee, the last time I saw him, proved to be just one such day. I remember taking a wrong turning on my way to the prison and passing a dead skunk surrounded by scavenging crows tearing at the remains. The smell emanating from the dead animal remained with me for a long time afterwards.

I remember parking Ward's car and passing all the checkpoints. I must have done everything according to the book and successfully passed the body search, but I have no memory of having done so. Nor do I recall much of what Pee-Wee and I talked about. I think that for much of the time we just sat and looked at each other without uttering a word.

We were both all too well aware that this was probably the last time we would see each other, though neither of us even hinted at such a thing. On the contrary, we did our best to appear cheerful.

'I'll come and see you in Norway when I qualify as a doctor,' Pee-Wee said. 'Then I'll take you fishing.'

'That'll be nice,' I answered limply.

The final minutes passed all too quickly. The guard came in to say that Pee-Wee had to be back in his cell in five minutes' time.

For the first time Pee-Wee put his fingers to his lips and pressed them against the glass that separated us, in a farewell kiss -- his first and last. Touched by his gesture, I did the same.

I knew instinctively that this would be my last visit to Texas.

***

A quarter of an hour after Robert White was declared dead, I made my way to the Burger King restaurant near The Walls. The girl behind the counter seemed unperturbed by the execution. She probably knew nothing about what had happened; executions were such a regular occurrence that they passed off with scarcely a ripple. In 1999, the year I was there, 98 people were put to death in the United States, 35 of them in Texas.[29] This was a peak year for executions

166

nationwide since lethal injections were reintroduced in 1976.[30]

In the little café, I set about collecting my thoughts about what I had just witnessed. I had been the first to arrive at The Walls, where White was to be executed. Feeling very much alone, I sat down on the ground, right in front of the entrance, but a guard told me to leave; they didn't want a demonstration that close to the prison. Members of the condemned man's family kept passing me on their way to the witness room; without exception, they were well groomed and nicely dressed. None of them vouchsafed me a glance. I had forgotten to bring my international press card with me, but I didn't really mind as I much preferred taking an active part in the demonstration.

The rest of the demonstrators joined me in ones and twos, to swell our number. For me, this was a first, but I gathered that most of the others were regulars; it was something they did quite often. My particular group comprised three women (Jacqueline, Carol and Jean), a married couple and an amiable professor from Sam Houston State University. They were all members of Amnesty and held aloft small Amnesty candles. My thoughts turned to Hal, but, unlike him, I didn't see anyone grilling.

The professor told us that he was a Catholic and that he deemed the death penalty fundamentally wrong.

Two of the women had that same day paid a visit to the women's prison at Gatesville. They claimed that prisoners there were stripped three times a day and that pepper was sprayed into their eyes. It was torture pure and simple, they said.[31]

Without warning, the television cameras focused on us. That was unusual, I gathered, but because Robert White had spent a longer time on Death Row than any other prisoner to date, his execution had attracted more attention than was customary.

The professor told reporters that he didn't think the media took their job seriously enough. All they were interested in, he said, was what the condemned men had for their last meal. He considered that to be a silly and irrelevant question.[32]

'It's despicable that that's the only thing that concerns you,' he said vehemently.

The professor went on to say that the media ought rather to concentrate on the actual procedure and the many mistakes that had been made over the years, and that White should instead have been sentenced to imprisonment for life.

Pee-Wee later wrote to me about my having taken part in the demonstration:

> Did you go to The Walls for the execution of Excell White? I know they killed him and I think he was ready to go.
> I know that it must have been an experience you won't forget any time soon, huh? How many people were there? I know there was a lot of people visiting from overseas.

It was six o'clock in the morning on 31 March 1999. I'd been awake for more than an hour, showered and dressed. I had packed my small rucksack and switched on the coffeemaker. I still had a few hours ahead of me before I needed to drive back to Houston, return the car to Ward and get to the airport. It was a daunting prospect and I couldn't help wondering whether I would manage it all.

I was still finding it hard to come to terms with Jacky and Charles's attitude to the death sentence. They had high ideals, there was no denying that, but they were simple people with simple answers to life's fundamental issues.

Just before I went to bed the previous evening Jacky had said to me:

'Let me ask you a question. If I'd been drunk and run you over, leaving you crippled for life, would you want me punished for what I had done?'

'Yes, of course I would,' I answered.

No more was said, but I continued to ponder the matter. I asked myself what if *I* had started smoking marihuana at nine, begun injecting drugs at thirteen, ended up on the street, a junkie, and, in a frantic hunt for money to fund my next dose, killed someone? Unable to imagine myself in such a situation in the first place, I had no answer, but I still thought that death was too severe a punishment – and most decidedly wrong.

Having dutifully made my $30 dollar donation to help in the upkeep of Hospitality House, I stole out and left Huntsville without seeing a soul.

A TURBULENT INTERLUDE

When I got back to Norway, I found a new letter from
Pee-Wee awaiting me:

> Thank you for the very loving visits. I truly
> enjoyed them but they went too fast and it
> seems like a dream. [. . .] I am almost finished
> with your clock. I've spent 13 hours just filling
> in the tooth-picks, that is the most time
> consuming [part] of making the whole clock.

I never received the wall clock he had spent so much
time making for me, but, as I have said, I had seen
similar clocks elsewhere, among them those in his
room in Hugo, so I know what it would have looked
like. He later confided in me that he had given it to his
youngest sister but never been thanked in return. One
day he wrote to me about his second cousin, the one
who had started him off injecting drugs when he was
thirteen.

> Do you remember I told you about my second
> cousin who first got me hooked on drugs?
> Well, he died of a heart attack in January. I
> learned that he was clean and sober and was
> counseling young people about drugs and that
> made me feel good because he'd cleaned his

act up and was helping someone doing the
right thing. [. . .] I don't get much mail at all, I
sit and wait like a dog waiting to be fed.
People don't understand the concept of death.
If they did, there would be no killing at all in
this world.
I have heard from my mother and she is
dying, she asked me not to tell my sisters and
brother. I don't think they care about me, I
have not seen any of them in 11 years. You
came twice from the other side of the world!
I have you in my life and you have been a
'true friend' to me.

In addition to his worries over his mother, Pee-Wee
was still striving to raise money for someone to take up
his case again and prove that he was innocent.

A fund his mother had started to this end had
turned out to be a great disappointment, as hardly any
money came in. One day, in the autumn of 1999, Pee-
Wee wrote me:

I am in need of a lot of money right now and
the only way I am going to have a chance of
getting a new trial is with money to hire the
investigators and experts I need. That is going
to take at least 11 000 dollars in order to
obtain the assistance, and time is of the
essence. I can't wait for my family to do
anything for me, I have to do it myself.

Eleven thousand dollars! Never in this world, I
thought, would he be able to raise such a sum.

In December of the same year I had a letter from Ward to say that he had been to see Pee-Wee and that they had talked a little about me. Ward had gained the impression that Pee-Wee had exaggerated expectations of what I could do for him, especially as regards starting a supportive fund in Europe. I remembered that Pee-Wee had mentioned something of the sort in one of his letters, though without asking for my help outright. I had replied that Norwegians weren't accustomed to that sort of thing and that in any case I had no idea of how to go about establishing such a fund.

Pee-Wee had told Ward that he had heard of several prisoners who had been helped to pay their legal fees by similar groups in Europe. Ward knew that money and political pressure from abroad had indeed helped a few prisoners, but he thought it unreasonable to expect that I personally could do anything similar.

***

The following year, 2000, was a turbulent time in my relations with Pee-Wee. Every time I received a letter from him it was to say that he had just mailed a letter to the authorities or his lawyer and that he still hadn't heard a word from his family. I didn't know what to say in reply – not to mention what to do.

I was finding it increasingly hard to continue our correspondence; as I pointed out to him, after seven years we had both changed. He had lost much of his old vigour and resilience, as was evident from his letters, and I, for my part, felt conscience-stricken by my growing tendency to put off writing to him. 18 January he put his feelings into words:

> This is about the seventh time I have started this letter to you. For some reason it's very, very difficult to write you. Ever since Ward entered our friendship, it has gone downhill.

I asked him what he meant by saying our friendship had gone downhill. I said that I thought it would be a sad thing if we were to lose contact after having corresponded for so long. I knew that I had begun to put off replying to his letters, but assured him that I always enjoyed hearing from him and invariably felt a tingle of excitement whenever I found one of those familiar long envelopes from Texas, many of them with small pencil drawings on the front, in my mailbox. I always wondered if anything out of the ordinary had happened, whether he had heard from the court or from his mother, or whether he was in one of his more philosophical moods. I never knew what to expect, apart from a lot about how hopeless the American legal system was, that he was innocent and that a key witness had lied.

Only ten days elapsed before I received a reply. The letter was written on high-grade notepaper, complete with a watermark depicting a palm-fringed beach. Pee-Wee was abject in his apology:

First of all I want to say this. I have nothing but UNCONDITIONAL LOVE in my heart for you and I mean that with all my heart. The reason I have difficulties writing to you at times isn't negative at all. I don't want to offend you in any kind of way and the last two letters that I have wrote (sic) you seem to think I'm mad at you or you take what I am saying the wrong way, so that is why I have difficulties at times writing to you. […] You know a lot about my case as does Korinna and that is because I put a whole bunch of trust in you and her, trust that I don't have for other people. […] I know of two other inmates here that all of a sudden started having problems with their friendships when Ward came into it. I don't think of Ward as a bad person, not at all. He has done a lot for me.
Marit, I haven't heard anything on my case as of this letter, but I will let you know as soon as I do.

On 17 February, a month after I had received Pee-Wee's letter, Ward emailed me to say that he had been to see Pee-Wee and that it had been a stormy encounter. Pee-Wee had been 'angry, unreasonable and egocentric to a degree'; he had also spoken disparagingly of a fellow prisoner. Ward was convinced that there was a reason for this sudden change of mood and that it was probably because a group in France had taken an interest in that particular inmate's case and raised enough money to get it reviewed.[33] It was this that was at the root of Pee-Wee's anger.

''Why can't someone help *me*?'' he'd wanted to know.
He made it plain that he thought Ward could have
done more to aid him.

Ward believed that Pee-Wee was also on edge
because he had still not heard anything about the
appeal he had lodged in 1997, more than two years
earlier.

Early in March 2000 Pee-Wee finally learned
the result of this last appeal. It was by no means the
one he had so earnestly hoped for. One week later I
received confirmation from Pee-Wee himself:

> The Court has denied my appeal and that
> means I will be getting an execution date. I
> don't know when that date will be, but it will
> be a serious date. I just don't understand how
> they can just deny everything without holding
> a hearing. It makes no sense to me at all.

He had been so sure that this time his appeal would
have been upheld.

In his next letter Pee-Wee reported that,
together with all the other men under sentence of
death at Ellis Unit, he had been transferred to a new
prison. From then on his letters regained much of
their former more upbeat tone:

> We have been moved to the Terrell Unit,
> actually it is now named Polunsky.

The move to Polunsky was a direct result of Martin Gurule's escape from Ellis Unit, as Polunsky was believed to be more secure.[34]

Although he continued to write about everyday matters, Pee-Wee definitely changed following the move. He lost interest in his surroundings and ceased drawing. More than once I had asked him if he would do a few drawings or write a verse or two for me, and now I asked him again. I thought it might take his mind off more morbid things. Only five days later, on 15 March 2000, I received his reply:

> Marit, it is very difficult to sit down and write poems and draw. It's not that easy any more. I have tried to do both but I just can't get into it. I have no hatred towards anyone, but I am very disappointed in my family. [. . .] To be very honest with you I am not afraid of dying but I don't want to die and pay for a crime that another person has committed. Anyway I need to change [the] subject because I get mad thinking of it.

Ward visited him again in April. Pee-Wee wrote that they had had a pleasant talk and that he had enjoyed a lot of junk food from a vending machine. There was a wider choice in the new prison, he said, and they could even buy sandwiches. Needless to say, it was Ward who paid.

The envelope was embellished with a drawing in Pee-Wee's characteristic style of a small dog, so at

least he had managed to draw something. Beneath the
drawing were these words: 'Take care of this doggie.'
In the accompanying letter he wrote:

> The little dog was my own idea. I had done it a
> long time ago and never sent it to you. I just
> can't sit down and draw any more because it's
> hard to focus on it. I have the same problems
> with writing poetry now. [. . .] My family isn't
> going to tell me anything about my mother.
> The last card I received from her she was very
> sick. I don't think anyone will tell her if I get a
> date. I know it will be on the news, but if I tell
> her now about my situation, it may make her
> worse.

I sent him a postcard to say that I knew that his appeal
had been turned down and how sorry I was. I
promised not to say anything to his mother, but felt
constrained to add that she was sure to learn about it if
a new date were to be set for his execution, as it would
be in every paper in Oklahoma and Texas.

Pee-Wee was at rock bottom, but in April 2000 something happened to give him renewed hope. At his insistent prompting, his lawyer had personally gone to see the prosecution's principal witness, the man who had told the court that Pee-Wee had admitted to him that he had committed the murder. *Now, unbelievably, the very same man, face to face with Pee-Wee's lawyer, confessed that he had lied.*

This last-minute admission might have made all the difference between life and death for Pee-Wee. It was, after all, this man's assertion that Pee-Wee had admitted to having killed Ms Denning that had tipped the scale and resulted in his being convicted of the murder.

The problem was that the man concerned adamantly refused to admit to the judge that he had lied in court, as he was afraid of being convicted of perjury and having his sentence prolonged after having lied to have it reduced. According to the newspaper cuttings I had read, he had been released from prison the day after giving testimony. In consequence, it was a matter of the witness's word against the lawyer's and, in the latter's opinion, the court was unlikely to set much store by any statement made by a man who had proved himself so untrustworthy. Be that as it may, the lawyer later wrote to me that 'at least it's something'.

I received this crumb of comfort in April 2000, but not until three weeks later did the lawyer inform Pee-Wee. Needless to say, I was surprised to learn that I had been told of the witness's confession before

Pee-Wee himself learned of it. This notwithstanding, when he was informed that the witness had admitted to having lied, for Pee-Wee it was like a shot in the arm. For years he had been saying that the man was lying and now, at long last, he hoped he would be believed.

> I have told this over and over, but no one would listen to me. I tried to get help to solve this case, but no one would help me. No one believed me.

But there was still the problem of how to get the man in question to admit before a court that he had lied. To this end, Pee-Wee immediately set about informing the authorities of this new turn of events and reading and rereading all the relevant documents.

Pee-Wee had regained his belief that his contention that he was innocent would be taken seriously. His lawyer, too, had grown more optimistic. In the past, Pee-Wee had repeatedly complained that he never heard from his lawyer, but now it seemed that the man had done a good job after all. For one thing, he urged me to write a letter in support of Pee-Wee for submission to the court. This I did. I wrote a four-page letter to the Texas Court of Criminal Appeals pleading for Pee-Wee's life. I sent it as an attachment to an email to the lawyer, who shortly afterwards wrote to thank me.

In a letter dated 19 May 2000 Pee-Wee wrote:

> I haven't heard from my lawyer lately, but my writ will be due in the Supreme Court in a few weeks and depending on what they do will depend on how much longer I have left to live. Something good has to happen, if they kill me, they will be killing an innocent man. I'm sure my lawyer has informed you what's going on.

Pee-Wee had heard nothing from his lawyer for several months, but now he wrote to say that he, the lawyer, had sent another request to the Supreme Court for a review of his case. In 1994 and 1995 Pee-Wee had himself appealed to the same court, but then his grounds had been weaker, as no new evidence had been forthcoming. Now it was different, as the reluctant witness's fresh confession had given him renewed hope. The question was, however whether the court would take due heed of what the man had said.

Not long afterwards Ward sent me an email to say that Stella had died on 23 July 2000. Three days later I received a letter in my mailbox from Pee-Wee to the same effect. (Prisoners were not allowed to exchange emails) It was not very revealing, however, as all he said in response to a question I had asked about his family was:

> I could have asked my mother but I regret to say that she died last Tuesday.

The brevity of his reply told me much about the depth
of his suffering and how he was suppressing his true
feelings, as I knew that he loved his mother more than
anyone. I felt terribly sorry for him but couldn't help
thinking that his parents would no longer remain
weighed down worrying about his fate. There was
nothing I could do other than send him my
condolences, which I did by return.

It was some months before I heard from him
again, but I knew that he was waiting for the Supreme
Court's decision on his appeal and assumed that his
reluctance to write was because his appeal had again
been dismissed. However, in the end, unable to
contain my impatience, I wrote and asked him why I
hadn't heard from him for so long. I told him a little
about my mother, whom I had recently visited in the
northern part of Norway, and who was still clinging to
life, though she could no longer speak and perhaps
didn't even know who we were.

I couldn't help wondering if he was displeased
with me for some reason, as in his last letter he had
seemed rather disgruntled and distant, though I was at
a loss to know why. It read:

> You don't know how difficult it is to wait and
> see what others decide to do with your life but
> I have always kept a positive mind during this
> whole period and that's very hard to do.

On 16 September 2000 I received the second and, as
it transpired, last email from Pee-Wee's lawyer.

It contained encouraging news – as far as it went. He wrote that he was still waiting for a decision from the Supreme Court but that the Texas Court of Criminal Appeals had agreed to consider an appeal for a new hearing. There was no means of knowing what the outcome would be, but whatever it was, it meant that Pee-Wee would not be given a new execution date within the immediate future.

I felt a surge of hope at this unexpected news. Might Pee-Wee's life be spared after all? And would the courts take into account the emergence of new evidence?

My hopes were soon dashed. On 30 October 2000, for the third time the Supreme Court refused to review Pee-Wee's case.

But still Pee-Wee wouldn't give up. On the contrary, from then onwards he redoubled his efforts to obtain a new hearing and appealed to a wide range of judicial institutions. It was to no avail: without exception, they refused to intervene.

After several months with only the odd letter now and then, to my surprise I received a small handwritten note from Pee-Wee. Dated 12 December 2000, it was written the same day that my third grandchild was born, which is why I remember it so well. In it, Pee-Wee thanked me for all I had done for him and wished me a happy Christmas. Then came the bombshell:

I'm out of your life now. The book deal you talked about, just throw it in the trash because that's where it belongs. Also, don't ask my lawyers about me or my case because I have told them not to talk to you or anyone else about it or me. You pushed me away from you and destroyed our friendship.

I was stunned! My first thought was that that was the end. I just couldn't take any more. Whatever's wrong with him? I wondered. I didn't know what to do.

In the envelope were more than fifty photographs I had sent him in the course of the seven years we had been corresponding. As I leafed through them, my whole life passed in review. There were photographs of my son's wedding in Spain, my first two grandchildren, my mother and the friendly fox that used to visit our holiday cabin; of sun-drenched Spanish beaches and my trip to China, everything; in short, of all that I had shared with him in close on eighty letters.

I was badly put out by the fact that he was prepared to end our long-standing friendship simply because he felt that I hadn't written often enough, though I couldn't help feeling sad at this sudden change in him, as he had come to mean a lot to me.

I later learned that Pee-Wee had also instructed his lawyer not to tell me how his case was going. He actually claimed that it was I who had alienated him and failed to keep my promises to him: 'You destroyed our friendship!' he said.

He said that he no longer wished to have anything to do with Ward either. In the end, however, it was Ward who provided what he thought was the explanation of this sudden and, in my view, uncalled-for outburst: that it was Pee-Wee's way of showing us that he felt both aggrieved and fearful. Ward said that, over the years, he had come to know a number of men under sentence of death and had realized that their anger was really an expression of their fear of what was to come. He thought we should simply wait for time to heal the breach. I sincerely hoped that he was right!

Prompted by Ward's explanation, I determined to write to Pee-Wee again, and in the interval between Christmas and New Year I sat down and wrote that I was sorry about the rift between us and expressed the hope that we could continue to correspond.

Pee-Wee replied immediately. In a letter dated 10 January 2001 he claimed that the cause of his outburst was that I had started writing to him so rarely and said that he had warned me that if I didn't write to him more often, he would return my photographs. I couldn't recall his ever having said anything to that effect, but to my chagrin, when I went through his more recent letters, I came across this:

> If I don't hear from you soon, I'll take that as a
> sign you no longer care to hear from me and
> I'll make sure you get your photos back.

I felt embarrassed at having overlooked something that meant so much to him, but I was annoyed by his threatening tone. He could have shown me more respect, I thought. What right had he to dictate when, and how often, I wrote? What entitled him to rule my life?

I had heard tell of prisoners who had threatened to withdraw their appeals unless their friends outside the prison showed more interest in their wellbeing. I consoled myself by reasoning that at least Pee-Wee hadn't gone that far but only chided me, albeit rather heartlessly, for my failure to reply promptly to his letters. As he himself said:

> I said I'd send your pictures back if I didn't hear from you, it surely was NOT an act of revenge, because if it would of (sic) been revenge, I'd tore all your photos up and thrown them away or sent them back that way.

It would have been foolish to end what was, in truth, a sincere and close friendship in such a manner, and I told him so. To my relief, he came round to my way of thinking and we resumed our correspondence almost as if nothing had happened. I sent him some new photographs, a gesture which he appeared to appreciate. Ward was similarly 'pardoned'. Pee-Wee put him back on his visitors list and, outwardly at least, returned to being his old self. The quarrel between us was never mentioned again, but more and more time began to elapse between letters, both his and mine. In

2001, for example, I received only six letters from Pee-Wee, while I wrote eight to him; this was far fewer than in the peak year of 1996, when I sent him 22.

Meanwhile, executions in the United States continued unabated. Eighty-five people were put to death nationwide in the year 2000, almost half of them (40) in Texas.[35]

I did my best to help Pee-Wee keep his spirits up and urged him to continue putting his thoughts down on paper. It didn't help:

> I don't have ink pens any more because they have taken them away from me, they were color pens and now I can't draw either. Anyway, those are only things and it isn't all that important.

In November 2001 I wrote to his younger sister Grace. This was only the second time I had written to her following my visit to Hugo seven years earlier. My first letter was to offer my condolences on the death of her mother, but I never received a reply. This time I wrote to implore her and her brother and sister to visit Pee-Wee as soon as they could, as he had just been allotted a new execution date: 16 January 2002.

According to Pee-Wee himself, this time there was little hope of a postponement. I replied that I was hoping for a miracle and said that he had always proved himself strong and courageous in the face of

186

adversity. I urged him to write if he felt up to it, but was careful to add that I fully understood if he didn't. I also asked him to phone me and reverse the charges, but he never did.

From then on, almost everything Pee-Wee wrote had to do with his case, so much so that he often repeated himself. I gathered that he had acquired more pen friends and had more visitors because of the publicity his case had aroused abroad. For some reason, Italians showed themselves extra strongly opposed to capital punishment, and not a few of them evinced interest in Pee-Wee. Several TV channels in Italy featured him in their programmes and the press had also taken up his impending execution, much to his gratification. Pee-Wee had always enjoyed being in the limelight. He once confided in me that he would have liked to have been a singer and that when he was small, he had made many stage appearances.

Pee-Wee no longer evinced the same urge for letters from me, which meant that I was able to relax more, though I still enjoyed hearing from him. I was very much aware that one day, perhaps in the very near future, our relationship would come to an end. I no longer thought it possible that he would avoid execution.

Shortly after writing to Grace, I heard from Pee-Wee again:

> I received a stay of execution on November 29, 2001. I was given an execution date on

October 09, 2001 for January 16, 2002. I
never give up hope on anything, I always think
positive and try to think only positive thoughts.
I got the stay from the Federal court, the 5th
Circuit of Appeals gave me permission to file
my writ of habeas corpus, and I can tell you,
they do not do that very often. I only know a
handful of inmates who have received that
type of relief, so now I just hope and pray that
I will finally get some relief. I have that feeling
deep down in my soul. With all that said, I still
have to prepare myself to die.
I got a letter from my brother, but it was just
because I had told him about the execution
date that was postponed. I also got a
Christmas card from Grace. She told me that
Jane had seen my lawyer on TV. He had
informed her about the new execution date.

In 2001, 66 people were executed in the United
States, 17 of them in Texas -- all in The Walls.[36]
Pee-Wee knew most of them, or knew who they were.
Two of those he was acquainted with had been in cells
adjacent to his.

Prisoners on Death Row usually developed a
kind of comradeship among themselves, and the closer
their execution date came, the more they tried to
encourage whoever's turn it was and help them to face
what lay ahead. Pee-Wee had told two of his
'neighbours', Jeffrey Tucker and Emerson Rudd,
when he bade them a last farewell, that they would be

going to a better place by far. 'Don't look upon it as dying,' he had said, 'but as a step towards a new and better world.'

> Both of my neighbors got executed last month. I watched as they both got on a van to the Walls unit and they never came back. If you don't want to go, they will force you to go and will do what they have to do to get you to the killing machines.

A TRANSFORMATION

On January 16 2002, I had a visit from a bishop in Italy, he has been supporting my case, anyway, when he came to visit he didn't have to be on my visitation list, so he got in through the chaplain's office. He gave me a personal letter from Pope John Paul II and a Blessed Rosary. It was a surprise and I couldn't believe it at first. You see, I am in fact a Catholic.

I was also surprised. The bishop's visit plainly meant a lot to Pee-Wee and he undoubtedly felt honoured by it. True, he had occasionally expressed a belief in God, but he had never struck me as being particularly religious – unless his musings on meditation and siddha-yoga could be considered religious. But what did I know? He may well have been born a Roman Catholic.

Two months later, on Good Friday, 29 March, he wrote:

I just paid for my trial records and now I can read and quote everything from the record and prove what I am talking about, plus I am in the process of getting some other records, so that I can show how I was treated and show I am innocent.

I truly feel I am going to win my freedom, I can feel it in my bones. I have to focus to save my life. I cannot let these people kill me for an act I did not commit, and I will fight to the bitter end.

I had still not got around to replying to this letter when, on 19 May, I received another letter from Pee-Wee:

I have not heard from you in a long time, so I thought I would drop in and see what has been going on in your world. It is always nice to find that out, but you don't write me as much as you used to, but you are a busy woman.

Following his stay of execution six months earlier, Pee-Wee had been given leave to lodge yet another appeal, but towards the end of July 2002 this too was denied.

But still he refused to give up. He wrote that he was going to mail me copies of all relevant documents, so that I could read everything for myself. He also promised to type out the parts he deemed most important:

I have been reading through my trial records and taking notes from that and I have found some interesting stuff, you see when you have the record in front of you, then you can quote from statement of facts, because that is what it is supposed to be, facts from the trial that people swore to tell the whole truth and

nothing but the truth. There is no evidence on
me to prove that I took part in this crime, the
only thing that links me to this crime is what
the jailhouse snitch said at my trial and his
word isn't any good. The state's prosecutors
told him what to say in court.

He said that he had found proof that the two police
officers who had witnessed against him had not spoken
the truth, though for some reason he failed to enlarge
on the matter. He was shocked, he said, to find that no
one, not even his lawyers, had spotted that the
testimony of these officers was flawed, for which
reason he was rereading all the documents with the
aid of a magnifying glass.

Pee-Wee went on to say that if he were
granted a new hearing, he would take the opportunity
this offered to cross-examine a number of witnesses.
He knew precisely what questions to pose, he said, and
intended to confront them with their lies:

> I am going to speak for myself, I'm intelligent
> enough to handle it. You see, I read law books
> and I fully understand the terminology and all
> that is going on, I read also the rules of the
> court so that I know what I can say now.

He found an old couple that wanted to help him
create a new web site. He had also been in touch with
the Houston branch of the Innocence Project, a non-
profit organization committed to getting wrongfully

convicted prisoners exonerated.[37] The organization
had taken up Pee-Wee's cause, which, he said, they
would not have done had they believed him guilty.

Pee-Wee was immensely grateful to all who
showed an interest in his case. He informed me that
he intended to publish all material documents on the
net.

It was not to be. Nothing came of the web site, and he
never said anything more about the Innocence
Project. I managed to write two long letters to him, the
first in June and the second, which was even longer, in
September. I told him how pleased I was that he was
still optimistic and full of hope, and thanked him for
the new documents he had sent me from the court
proceedings. I sincerely hoped that he would be
granted another hearing.

I told him about the fine summer weather we
were having and brought him up to date on family
affairs, including the death of my mother on 20
October. In his reply he wrote:

> You know, I had a strong feeling that your
> mother was dead and I even started on a letter
> to ask, but was afraid it would make you sad
> and I might have been wrong. My
> condolences to you and your family.

The year my mother died, 2002, 69 men and two
women were executed in the United States; 33 of the
men were given lethal injections in Texas.[38]

13 April 2003:

> Thank you for your long, handwritten letter. It must have taken you a while to write it, so thank you. You know that I don't get many handwritten letters like that, so I appreciate it. I wish my parents were still alive. The only thing that really gets to me is not being able to go to their funeral and pay my final respects. They took that away from me and there is nothing in this world they could give me to bring that back or make up for it.

14 July 2003:

> You ask about my case. Well, the court denied my appeal on May 01, 2003 and it doesn't look too good right now. It is possible that I will be getting an execution date soon. I have until the end of this month to file my writ to the Supreme Court and whatever they do will decide if I get a date or not, but to me it really doesn't matter one way or the other.

On 18 July Pee-Wee's lawyers lodged a fourth application with the Texas Supreme Court for a review of his case, along with a request for a new appraisal of the decisions handed down by lower courts.

On 6 October 2003 this application was turned down, which meant that, unless he were granted a last-minute reprieve, there was no longer any hope of Pee-Wee's having his sentence commuted. The chance of a reprieve was very small; it was many years since a prisoner had been reprieved in Texas.

I just can't understand how they can deny me
a new hearing after all the documents I have
submitted. It makes no sense. I appreciate that
you don't tell my family that the court denied
my application. It doesn't actually matter what
happens. If I die, well, I will not be here any
more. If I get a final date, I will not write to
anyone again. I feel it will just be worse for
others, and I do not want to bother people
with my situation.

I can tell you that I have lost some weight
since you saw me. I do some training every
day in order to keep in shape. Worrying just
keeps you away from real freedom.
I have already made preparations for my
funeral if I get executed. I have already paid
for it so there will be no expenses and suchlike
for my family.

A month later, on 29 October, a date was finally set
for Pee-Wee's execution: 4 December that same year.

LAST LETTERS

The prospect of Pee-Wee's imminent execution left me in a quandary. I didn't know what to say to him, but I felt I had to say something.

In my next-to-last letter to him, which was dated 6 November 2003, I thanked him for our long friendship and told him how greatly I admired him for his courage, inner calm and concern for others. Shortly afterwards, on 17 November, I wrote again to say that I hoped his life would be saved by a last-minute miracle. I found it impossible to express my true feelings. I calculated that in the course of the ten years we had been in correspondence I had sent him 102 letters, as well as numerous postcards.

On 19 November, a few days before my letter reached him, Pee-Wee wrote what was to prove his last letter to me, number 115, to thank me for our sincere and enduring friendship:

> Dear Marit, Well, as of the writing of this letter I haven't received a stay, but I haven't given up hope either. Anyway, I am just taking things one day at a time and I've decided that since I was receiving such a huge number of letters of support from around the world, I would answer some of them and let people know how much I appreciate their caring and very loving support.

I haven't heard from any of my family. I made my own funeral arrangements two days ago.

It will be a long time before I will get any rest, because I have to go to the main office tomorrow morning and give them all the information they will need to carry out their job. I will have to give them a list of five people who will witness my execution, my request for a final meal, the clothes that I will wear, say if I will make a final statement and if I want to have a spiritual advisor there to witness my execution. Also who will claim my body, as if it were just trash. Things like that will be the topic of our conversation in the morning.

For the first time he wrote about his daughter, the little girl in a white-lace dress whose photograph I had seen on the wall of Stella's house in Hugo:

I have no idea where my daughter is, or her mother. I wish I did, because I would like to talk to her myself and let her know how I was railroaded, then she could be a voice for me. I don't know what she has been told about me, but I'm sure she has been told things and she probably doesn't know that I have tried very hard to get in touch with her.

I wish I could share more of my poetry with you and drawings, but it is very difficult to sit down and focus on that now.

I feel the same as you do. You have been a
great friend to me and done a lot for me when
you were able to, and I am grateful for that. I
know you would have liked to have done
more, but I'm not complaining. You really
didn't need to do anything at all so I'm very
glad to have had a friend like you. I only wish
I could have given you more of myself. Some
people have an easier path through life than
others. Mine was all pain and misery. I have
fought my way through many things. When I
look back I realize that I never had any really
true friends when I was young. A true friend
picks you up when you stumble and fall.

When I was a drug addict, none of my friends
were there to say we care for you and you are
ruining your life with that stuff. My parents
told me before to leave it alone, but with
parents it is different, the more they talk to me
the more I rebelled against them. I hid my
drug problems from my parents. Had my
mother known that it was my second cousin
who stuck that needle in my arm at the age of
13, she would have killed him.

Marit, I'll stop here and put this letter in the
mail to you. I hope you have a nice day and
remember: I love you very much.

Your own Ivan Ray.

He had said that he wouldn't be writing to anyone
now that a definite date for his execution had been set,

but in the event he wrote to his faithful pen-friends to
let us know how he was coping. I was deeply sorry
about my inability to do anything to comfort him
other than to write him yet another letter. I still don't
know if it reached him in time.

THE COUNTDOWN

Pee-Wee's execution was scheduled to take place at six o'clock in the evening on Thursday, 4 December 2003. Texas time was seven hours behind Norwegian time, meaning that in Oslo it would be night. Ahead of me lay a long and agonizing vigil.

***

A number of us made one last try to obtain for Pee-Wee a reprieve or, failing that, a stay of execution. Korinna, for one, petitioned the governor of Texas, Rick Perry, and the Texas Board of Pardons and Paroles, and a friend of mine, Turid Ihle, who had worked hard to have the death penalty abolished, did the same. Amnesty International lodged an appeal, as they always did, and Ward appealed on behalf of the TCADP. I too had written to Perry.

But Ward had done more. He had published an open letter on the Internet in which he claimed that there was no evidence that Pee-Wee had killed Ms Denning. The only evidence the state had for executing him was a statement by an informant, a fellow prisoner, who later confessed that he had lied. He went on to say that if PeeWee had been able to pay for his own defence, he would probably never have received the death penalty in the first place.

200

If Pee-Wee had been able to pay for his own defence,
he would probably never have received the death
penalty in the first place. In Ward's opinion this
should have been a decisive factor and resulted in a
postponement.

It was not to be. Despite our concerted pleas, there
was no prospect of a respite. I knew that Pee-Wee's
chances were growing slimmer with every hour that
passed. Six men were to be executed in Texas between
3 and 12 December and all the preliminaries had been
carried out; for the prison authorities, executions were
routine.

As was his privilege, Pee-Wee had informed the
staff of what he would like for his last meal and also of
what his last words would be. He was entitled to name
five people to witness his execution, but whether he
availed himself of this right I do not know. I do know,
however, what he chose for his last meal: fried
chicken, fried fish, fried pork chops, French fries, fried
onion rings, tomato ketchup and tartar sauce.[39]

I couldn't help thinking of all the hapless men
and women who had proceeded Pee-Wee on their
way to the death chamber and of their grieving
relatives gathered outside The Walls: mothers, fathers,
sisters, brothers, children. They may not have been
there so often in the past, but on this, the condemned
man's last day on earth, all had made an extra effort
to be present.

I was eager to see whether any of Pee-Wee's relatives
would attend. I thought it unlikely. My thoughts

turned to Jane, Grace and Pee-Wee's younger brother, and to how heart-rending these last hours must be for them, even though it meant an end to their years of suffering. Pee-Wee was thirty-eight years old and had spent the last twelve and a half years of his life on Death Row; I had known him for ten of those years. I couldn't help wondering if he would make a last-minute confession, but thought it most unlikely.

Ward had told me that he was expecting a postponement to be announced on Monday 1 December as another prisoner, a man by the name of Robertson, who was in much the same position as Pee-Wee, had recently been granted a stay of execution. I checked my incoming emails to see if there was any news from Texas, but to no avail: there wasn't a word either way,

On 2 December Ward mailed me again:

> The court has obviously not taken any notice of the Robertson case or Ivan's appeals. Unless a genuine miracle occurs, there's nothing to stop Ivan's scheduled December 4 execution. It's terrible.

Korinna, who had flown over to Texas, emailed me to say that she intended to witness the execution seventeen hours later. She said that Pee-Wee had promised her that he would give her a farewell smile

when he was strapped down on the gurney. She had
been granted special permission to spend eight hours
together with him outside the 'cage' on two successive
days, and she told me that the two of them had had
some rewarding conversations. She planned to join
Pee-Wee for four hours on his last morning too and
said that, if I liked, I could send her a few farewell
words that she would pass on to him.

She said Pee-Wee seemed to have come to
terms with his fate. He was still positive and neither
angry nor embittered; but he was deeply disappointed
that none of his family had been to visit him. Korinna
said she had phoned his brother and both his sisters
and almost begged them to come. She had even
offered to pay for a car and cover their other expenses,
but none of them felt they could face the ordeal.

Pee-Wee had received a lot of letters from all
over the world and Korinna thought they had helped
buoy him up. She herself had repeatedly phoned Pee-
Wee's lawyer to learn the result of his appeal to the
Texas Board of Pardons and Paroles, but had never
managed to get hold of him. In the end it was his
secretary who informed her that the appeal had been
dismissed; it was left to Korinna to tell Pee-Wee,
which she thought was outrageous. After all, she said,
it was the lawyer's duty to inform his client of the
outcome of his appeal and there was no excuse for his
not having done so.

She also wrote: He receives every day a whole
bunch of letters and they also cheer him up. There are
many

people out there in the world who think of him
at the moment and especially on Thursday. I
think he will be guided and held up by so
many thoughts and candle lights, they will
make the step into the other world easier.

I wrote back immediately to say how much I admired
her for all she had done for Pee-Wee and to ask her to
inform him of the many appeals for clemency that had
been lodged on his behalf. I also asked her to tell him
that my thoughts were with him.

On 4 December at 16.51 (almost two hours before it
should happen) Ward sent me another email headed
'Extremely Bad News':

> I met Korinna last night. It was the execution
> vigil for Richard Duncan. Korinna and I
> talked for an hour or so afterwards. I told her
> that I will be there tonight also. After it's over
> she can come down the hill to the vigil area.
> Although I have witnessed two executions, I'm
> unable to prepare her for it.
>
> I was glad Ivan had someone to be with the
> last couple of days.

***

My husband and I had earlier agreed to attend a
friend's pre-Christmas party in Oslo on the evening of

4 December. I felt duty bound to go, but was unusually quiet all evening: I couldn't help thinking of what was taking place at the same time in Texas. I was careful not to voice my thoughts, however, as I had no wish to spoil the party, but when we felt we decently could, we made our excuses and left early.

When we got home, my husband suggested that we should light two candles. That done, we sat down to wait. It never occurred to us to switch on the television or to pick up a book; we didn't even talk.

As the clock moved inexorably closer to one, we knew that the decisive moment was imminent. We were still dozing in our chairs when Korinna rang. It was two o'clock in the morning on 5 December. She was very agitated and barely able to speak. I was immensely grateful to Pee-Wee for not asking me to witness his execution. He had never told me that he had asked Korinna to be present.

In the event, no one from Pee-Wee's family attended his execution, but on his last day he had long conversations over the phone with his brother and two sisters. Korinna said that, afterwards, a strange calm seemed to have descended on him. She also said that he appeared to have resigned himself to his fate and was prepared to let the law take its course.

She admitted that it had been a trying experience altogether, though Pee-Wee himself had behaved in exemplary fashion.

She had caught his eye and he had kept his promise and given her a wry smile.

In the official account of his execution it was stated that twenty minutes elapsed before he was declared dead.

How does one feel on being informed that someone one knew has been executed? I think the nearest I can get is numbed, though helpless may be nearer the mark; angry, too, maybe. I just don't know, but I do know that I found myself unable to shed a tear: deep down, I felt relieved that at long last Pee-Wee's years of hoping and suffering were over.

Although it was the middle of the night, I set about tidying the cushions on the sofa, washed our two coffee cups and watered a few potted plants.

The day after Pee-Wee's execution, I had another email from Ward:

> Korinna witnessed the execution. Afterwards there was a funeral mass at the Huntsville Funeral Home.
> I guess that Ivan was either Catholic, or he converted to Catholicism. Three Catholic priests were there. At least one of the priests had come directly from Rome. I was uncomfortable with the ceremony and the ritual of the mass, but I feel that the funeral

mass was something that was important to Ivan. No one from Ivan's family came -- in fact, they all stayed in Oklahoma. Ivan was allowed to telephone them Thursday afternoon. From all reports his phone conversation with them went well.

Later the same day I received an email from Dennis Longmire, one of the many people who had involved themselves in the closing stages of Pee-Wee's case:

> It is nine p.m. and I come straight from a mass held to commemorate Ivan's life. He had been asked by the warden: How was your day, Ivan? His answer was: Warden, today was a beautiful day.

Pee-Wee's last words found their way into the newspapers. The victim's relatives dismissed them as 'religious claptrap', as Pee-Wee had placed himself in the hands of God. His last words were:

> I would like to thank everybody for coming out tonight and celebrating life. This is a celebration of life, not death. Through Jesus Christ, we have victory over death. I would like to thank the Holy Father and Pope John Paul for their angelic blessings and all the prayers and support. And thanks to Father Guido Todeschini for your love and support. I want to thank everybody around the

world and Father, let your will be done. I am
going to keep this statement short. I love you
all. I am ready, Warden.

Although this was very unlike Pee-Wee, I realized how
much he had changed after languishing for so many
years in prison. In a way, he had had his fill of life.

Dennis continued:
I didn't know Ivan personally, but I know that
his spirit touched a lot of people, and the best
that happened was his farewell to the family
before he was set free. In my ears I still have
the echo of Bob Dylan's *I shall be released* after I
heard Ivan's declaration that he was innocent:

*'Down here next to me in this lonely crowd, is a man
who says he's not to blame. All day long I hear him cry
so loud, calling out that he's been framed. I see my light
come shining, from the west down to the east. Any day
now, any day now, I shall be released.'*

The same year, 2003, 65 people were executed in the
United States, 24 of them in Texas. Pee-Wee, the
sixty-fourth of them, was next to last. His prison
number was 989, but he died as number 884 as the
death penalty was reintroduced in 1976.[40]

***

Unable to help myself, two days after Pee-Wee's execution I wrote a joint letter to his brother and sisters. I began by expressing my condolences and went on to say how pleased I was that they had all spoken to him on his last day. I concluded by saying that they should never be ashamed of their brother. I said that he had been a good man at heart but had taken a wrong path in life and that I knew he loved each and every one of them. I also told them how much Pee-Wee had meant to me personally. I sent the letter by regular mail, as I had all the letters I had sent Pee-Wee in the course of our ten-year correspondence.

I never received an answer, but I didn't expect one either. A few days later I had a long conversation over the phone with Korinna, who was still in America. We agreed that I should visit her in Switzerland early in the new year to talk things over; after all, Pee-Wee had been a mutual friend.

I made good on my promise in 2004. I stayed with Korinna for three days and the two of us shared our experiences as friends of a man who had been executed. Korinna told me in detail what, for the first and, she fervently hoped, last time it had been like to see a man she knew put to death. She had brought some of Pee-Wee's belongings back with her to Switzerland. Among them were all the documents relating to his case, photographs and letters from the two of us, along with the clothes he had worn. His address book contained the names of pen friends all over the world; there were many from Switzerland and, in addition to those from me, a few from Norway.

Neither of us could suppress a smile when Korinna drew out a large pair of white underpants. These few oddments apart, Pee-Wee had meticulously cleared everything away before he left this world for good.

EPILOGUE

Over twenty-four years have passed since I received my first letter from Pee-Wee and fourteen since he died. I still don't know whether or not he was guilty of murder, but if he was innocent, it makes it extra hard for me to come to terms with his having been executed.

I often think of him and what his friendship meant to me. Corresponding with a man on Death Row can be extremely demanding, but it also begets many happy moments and rewarding experiences. I have never regretted our relationship, but it was a one-off: never again will I enter into correspondence with a person in the same situation.

Many people have asked me, as I have asked myself, why I took so long to write about my friendship with Pee-Wee. The answer is, quite simply, that I started jotting down snatches here and there while the two of us were still writing to each other, but as our friendship evolved and Pee-Wee fought ever harder for his life, I found myself unable to go on writing. The two of us had grown too close. All our letters, both his and mine, were filed away to gather dust – a well-preserved secret.

In February 2014, 11 years after Pee-Wee's death, I wrote to Ward to ask if anything new had emerged relevant to Pee-Wee's case. He wrote back to say that nothing had and that it was seldom that new facts came to light following an execution. He also said that he was still visiting prisoners under sentence of death in Texas, but not as often as in the past.

Nonetheless, Ward expressed renewed interest in Pee-Wee's case when he learned that I was contemplating writing a book about it. In February that same year he visited the National Archives in Texas and made copies of all the court proceedings and appeals, together with the subsequent denials. After going through them all, in March 2014 he wrote to me:

> It sure appears to me that (with a proper appeal) Ivan should not have been executed on Dec 4, 2003. It also sure appears to me that his lawyer did an absolutely terrible job for Ivan. I hadn't dealt with Ivan for a few years prior to his execution, so I wasn't aware of the exact details and that last appeal.

He then went on to say:

> Also, Ivan's death sentence (but not the conviction) should have been overturned. The Grayson county prosecutor would most likely have tried to re-sentence Ivan to death. Who knows what would have happened? Ivan could have gotten a new death sentence, or he could have been sentenced to life in prison. Even if he didn't actually kill Lula Mae Denning

himself, Ivan was guilty of being a criminal
part of that murder. Laws in Texas are very
broad regarding the culpability of criminal
accomplices.

Even now, after all these years, I remain in doubt
about Pee-Wee's guilt. I hate to think that he beat a
poor, defenceless old woman to death. I prefer to
believe that he fled in panic when he realized what
was about to happen and that he was speaking the
truth when he claimed that he had not been
responsible for killing her. Neither I nor anyone else
will ever know what actually happened.

The uncertainty involved in not knowing all the
facts is one of the many reasons why capital
punishment is so iniquitous, regardless of the matter of
guilt.
Like Ward, I too have made a careful study of Pee-
Wee's criminal record.

At the age of eighteen, in September 1983, the
Texas Department of Criminal Justice imposed a
suspended three-year sentence for theft. On 6
September 1984 this was changed to unconditional
imprisonment and two months later he was ordered to
serve the original three years in prison. He was
released on parole in Oklahoma in May 1985 but only
a year later, in May 1986, he was sentenced to four
years in the state prison after having admitted to
having received stolen gods in Choctaw County,
Oklahoma. In September 1986 he was sentenced to
two years' imprisonment in Oklahoma for stealing two

cars. Then, on 30 June 1989, again in Oklahoma, he was sentenced to two seven-year terms in prison for shooting with intent to kill.[41]

***

Although I was responsible for bringing Pee-Wee to the notice of the world at large, it was he who was the more open of us. As far as I could judge, he held little, if anything, back, be it his likes and dislikes or his joys and hates. Some people may think of him as manipulative. I prefer to see him as forthright and sincere. I am convinced that writing to me was, for him, a kind of therapy, as was writing to Korinna and many others. I know that he had other correspondents besides Korinna and myself, but he made me, at least, feel that I was the only one.

Korinna and I are still in touch with each other, though not as often as in the past. We are agreed that Pee-Wee meant a lot to us both and that, with the exception of his family, she and I were the ones who meant most to him. I asked Korinna if she still thought him innocent. She had always been convinced that it wasn't Pee-Wee who had killed Lula Mae Denning. She had read all the relevant documents and felt that a lot of mistakes had been made. Now, however, she was not so sure and thought he might have been guilty after all, or at least been there.

My mind occasionally goes back to what Amnesty wrote in their first letter to me – that

214

prisoners like Pee-Wee, living under sentence of death, were widely regarded as the scum of society.

I would love to meet Pee-Wee's daughter and tell her that I never looked upon her father as the monster many people made him out to be. Unfortunately I know nothing about her and I doubt whether I shall ever find her. The only thing I know about her for certain is that she was born in 1986 and that her mother was Pee-Wee's girlfriend; that I have from the court records.[42]

***

Conditions on Death Row in Polunsky Unit are much the same now as they were in Pee-Wee's time, though according to information I have recently received, they may have worsened. Nowadays, people visiting prisoners under sentence of death are allowed only two hours with them, though in exceptional cases this can be extended to eight. Prisoners are confined to their cells for twenty-three hours a day, which is two hours longer than when Pee-Wee was there. The food is said to be poorer and cells are often dirty and untidy. Some prisoners become psychotic, as they are unable to cope with so many years of solitary confinement. At ninety-day intervals, give or take a day or two, there is what is known as a lockdown, followed by a shakedown, when all the prisoners' belongings are subjected to a thorough search. The prisoners themselves undergo body searches even though they are never in physical contact with anyone other than the guards.

Whenever they are outside their cells, inmates are handcuffed and some even have their feet manacled. With a guard on either side, they have no possibility of smuggling anything into their cells. Mail is censored and all are regularly woken up at three every morning to be counted.

I understand that there have been far fewer visitors from abroad to the Polunsky Unit in recent years and that there are more empty seats in the Visitors Room than when I was there. This may be attributable to the downturn in the world economy, but several people have commented on the oppressive atmosphere that seems to dominate the chamber. Many prisoners have been transferred to other states, where conditions are rumoured to be better.[43]

Eighty per cent of prisoners on Death Row in America who express a wish for pen friends are women, many of them very young.[44] This notwithstanding, in summer 2000 Amnesty discontinued its practice of putting prisoners in touch with people outside, as the Internet was increasingly taking over. Nowadays, people all over the world have their own special prisoner, with whom they correspond via the net. Prisoners on Death Row do not have Internet access but are helped to maintain contact with well-wishers by relatives and friends. It is now possible to send emails to JPay, a US-based, corrections-related service that passes on copies of letters to prisoners.[45]

216

In 1972 the US government introduced a nationwide moratorium on the death penalty, which put an end to executions for the next four years. Gary Gilmore made world headlines in 1977 when the death penalty was reintroduced and he was executed by firing squad. Gilmore was the only person to be put to death that year.[46] From 1 January 1988 through 29 April 2014, 1,379 people were executed in the United States.[47]

As of 1 October 2013, 3,088 people were in prison in America awaiting execution, 287 of them in Texas.[48] When this book was written, there were 741 prisoners on Death Row in California. However, since 1977 'only' 13 have been executed and none have been put to death since 2006, when one man was executed. In 2013, 80 people were sentenced to death in the United States.[49]

It is encouraging to note that the number of executions has fallen in recent years. In 2003, the year Pee-Wee died, 65 people were executed in America, 24 (37 per cent) of them in Texas. Ten years later, in 2013, 'only' 39 people were executed nationwide, with Texas again topping the list at 16 executions (41 per cent). That year, 32 states still had the death penalty on their statute books, but only nine of them actually carried out an execution. In the course of the last six years, that is, up to 2013, six states have abolished the death penalty.

The decline in executions notwithstanding, the majority of Americans remain in favour of the death penalty, though their number is steadily decreasing. In 1996 execution was still favoured by 78 per cent of the population, and as late as 2014, 55 per cent were still in favour. The situation is improving, however: when people are offered a choice between death and imprisonment for life with no possibility of parole, the percentage in favour of execution falls to 50.[50]

Another encouraging development is provided by the restrictions governing who is liable for execution. It is now against the law to sentence to death a person who is mentally handicapped, and people who commit murder before they reach the age of 18 are also exempted. Another welcome improvement is that prosecutors are no longer entitled to debar non-whites from serving on juries.[51]

In spite of these advances, the fact remains that prospective jury members still have to testify that they are not opposed to the death penalty. This, of course, excludes many prospective jurors.[52]

From 1973 to 2014, 144 men and women under sentence of death in the United States have been granted a reprieve. The last of them was Glenn Ford from Louisiana, who was released in March 2014 with the emergence of new evidence to prove that he had been wrongfully convicted of murder. By then he had spent 30 years in prison under constant threat of execution.[53] It is interesting to note that of the 144 men and women reprieved, 18 were freed following DNA tests.

Pee-Wee never had this option as, in his day, DNA testing was still in its infancy. Interestingly, as this book goes to press in 2017 (the 1st edition was published in Norwegian in 2014), murder rates are again rising in America's principal cities.

***

Stella once remarked to me that the whole family was under sentence of death -- which does much to explain why they were all so keen that his story should be brought to the notice of a wider public.

In the winter of 2014 I found a photograph of Pee-Wee's grave on the Internet. He was buried in Springs Chapel cemetery in Choctaw County, Oklahoma, in a plot close to his parents' graves. His father, Ivan Sr, died at the age of 59 on 7 May 1988 and Stella, his mother, on 23 July 2000 when she was 54.

His siblings elected to disregard Pee-Wee's wish that his ashes should be scattered somewhere in Europe, whose people had, he felt, done most to help him. On the other hand, thanks to them he wasn't cremated and his ashes interred amid the many nameless wooden crosses, marked only by a number, that dot the prison graveyard in Huntsville. His brother and two sisters gave him a proper funeral. He was buried dressed in a light-blue Dallas Mavericks basketball shirt and black trousers with a rosary in his hand.

Shortly after he died, one of his sisters told Korinna that they intended to have inscribed on his gravestone 'Killed by the State of Texas'. Nothing came of this idea, however, and Pee-Wee's gravestone bears the more conventional inscription: 'Forever in our hearts. Ivan Ray Murphy Jr. Jan. 10, 1965 – Dec. 4, 2003.' On each side of the inscription is a leaping fish. Beneath, in capital letters, are these two words:

GONE FISHING

ACKNOWLEDGEMENTS

I wrote this book primarily in memory of my friend Ivan Ray Murphy Jr, aka Pee-Wee. He was never able to read it, but at least I have kept the promise I once made to him that I would write it.

I am indebted to many people for helping me in the process.

First and foremost I wish to thank Pee-Wee's family in Oklahoma for their unstinting help and hospitality. My thanks are also due to Ward Larkin for so often visiting Pee-Wee and working so hard to have the death penalty abolished and for much invaluable information. I am likewise grateful to Juliane Victoria (Turid) Ihle for all she too has done to put an end to capital punishment in America and to Korinna Hofheinz, who stood by Pee-Wee to the end. I am similarly indebted to Jon Trana and John Peder Egenæs of Amnesty International Norway, and to Lill Scherdin, who taught me a lot about the US appeals system; and to Heidi Vindenes for updating me on conditions on Death Row in Texas. I should also like to thank George McFarland ('Big George'), who was condemned to death in 1992 and is still (2017) on Death Row in Texas.

I am also very grateful to Kamilla Simonnes of
Manifest Publishing for her help with the Norwegian
edition of this book.

Furthermore I wish to thank the young artist Emilio
Nathaniel Taveras for his wonderful fantasy drawing
of Pee-Wee fishing.

222

My thanks are also due to *The Norwegian Nonfiction Writers and Translators Association* for enabling me to write the book in Norwegian. I also wish to thank my friend J. Basil Cowlishaw for translating the book into English.

Above all I am grateful to my husband Eivind for his helpful advice, constructive criticism and, not least, forbearance while I was writing this book.

In the interests of those concerned, I have changed the names of some of the persons who appear in this book.

AFTERWORD

John Peder Egenæs
Secretary General, Amnesty International Norway

When a civilized state such as the USA sets out to execute someone, it helps if the person concerned can be personified as a heartless monster. We constantly see examples of this, both in law reports and in the media's coverage of court proceedings that conclude with a death sentence. Demonization of the perpetrators is very much the rule. I am personally acquainted with a man who was once subjected to such extreme vilification.

This was Kerry Cook, who spent twenty-two years on Death Row before being released. He had been condemned to death for rape and murder and held in prison despite repeated appeals; each time he was forced to hear the prosecuting attorney refer to him as 'a perverse madman and cannibal', words which also appeared in press reports of the proceedings. Since his release as a result of DNA tests that proved that he was not the person responsible, Cook has devoted all his time and effort to trying to convince people that he was not at all the monster he was made out to be. With the aid of a book, numerous lectures, plays and, finally, a film, Cook has painted an entirely different picture of himself and many of the

men incarcerated with him on Death Row: a picture
of human beings.

It is not only the wrongfully convicted who
deserve to have their stories told: also the guilty are
human beings with a story that is much longer and
more multifaceted than the description of their crimes
would suggest. In many cases, after sentence has been
passed, jury members have declared that had they
been made acquainted with the accused person's
whole story, they would never have voted for the
death sentence.

In court, recounting a person's life story is often
ruled as inadmissible, generally because the accused's
defence counsel is so lackadaisical or downright
incompetent that such extenuating circumstances as
may exist are never brought to the attention of the
court. The consequence is that prosecutors are able to
demonize and dehumanize a person without restraint.
This both edges the accused ever closer to execution
and strengthens universal support for the death
penalty. All humane considerations are relentlessly
swept aside.

It is precisely for these reasons that books like
this one are so important. Whether he was innocent,
as he claimed to be, or guilty, Murphy was first and
foremost a human being, a man with his own personal
strengths and weaknesses, dreams and aspirations. In
all probability readers will sometimes find themselves
agreeing with him, at other times totally at variance
with his conduct and opinions, just as they do with
other people they meet or read about.

In the mid-1990s, when Murphy was in prison, for several years in succession more than three hundred men and women were sentenced to death in the United States following reintroduction of the death penalty in 1977, when 98 people were executed. Fortunately, since then matters have improved somewhat, as from the year 2000 onwards the number of death sentences and executions has fallen slightly. In 2013, for example, 39 people were executed, but that same year 'only' 80 people were condemned to death, the lowest number since 1977.

In the interim, the pros and cons of capital punishment were hotly debated in an increasing number of states, and in six states the death penalty was abolished. At the time of writing, the death penalty is still on the statute books of 32 states, but only a few of these continue to practise it.

There are undoubtedly a number of reasons why death sentences and executions are still on the decline. One of them is the incidence of crime in the various states. According to the Death Penalty Information Center, murder rates in the US have consistently fallen over the last ten years. This notwithstanding, the southern states, which regularly top the execution statistics, still rank highest in regard to murder rates.   However, more and more people are asking themselves whether putting people to death has any appreciable effect and whether it does anything to protect the average law-abiding America citizen against falling victim to violent crime. That it does have an effect has always been a mainstay of the

pro-execution lobby, though no convincing empirical
evidence for such an assumption has so far been
forthcoming.

Another important reason for the ongoing
decline in support for the death penalty is that, in
recent years, no fewer than 144 people under sentence
of death have been released when it was found that
they were innocent and had been wrongfully
convicted. This has prompted politicians and many
members of the general public to face up to the fact
that the death penalty, like the laws relating to it, is
badly flawed and that not a few innocent men and
women have been executed as a result. A minor point,
one that is more a matter of principle, is that,
especially in the years when the United States was in
the throes of an economic crisis, the cost of putting a
person to death far outweighed that of keeping people
in prison for life. Life imprisonment costs far less than
mounting a trial culminating in execution.

In the course of the last few years, much
attention has been focused on methods of execution,
and many people have begun to question whether
they wish to be a party to such barbaric procedures.
All the American states that still practise execution
now do so by lethal injection as opposed to hanging,
shooting and the electric chair, some of which
methods are manifestly less humane than others. In
actual fact it is impossible to say whether one
particular method is more humane than another,
however, as no one lives to tell the tale. On not a few
occasions people executed by lethal injection have

made it plain as they were dying that they were in pain or suffering in other ways.

The US Constitution prohibits the imposition of 'cruel or unusual' punishments, with the consequence that there have been a number of cases in which defence lawyers have endeavoured to convince courts that death by lethal injection is very much a 'cruel' punishment.

In addition to these more practical reasons for the decline in support for capital punishment is the fact that, by and large, Americans are changing their views on execution. A poll in 2010 revealed that only 33 per cent of the population deemed the death penalty justified for murder. This is a nationwide figure and in consequence reflects the opinions of people resident in states that no longer execute people. It may safely be assumed that support for the death penalty is greater in states that still practise it, though revenge as a motive may be losing support. An important factor is that imprisonment for life makes it possible to rectify matters if it is subsequently found that a person has been wrongfully convicted. In the mid-1990s, some 85 per cent of Americans declared themselves in favour of the death penalty.

Over the last ten years, the US Supreme Court has handed down a series of rulings that suggest that a new conception of law is slowly gaining ground. In 2002, for example, the Court ruled that it was unconstitutional to condemn a mentally handicapped person to death, and in 2005 the Court determined that it was equally unconstitutional to condemn a minor to death. This means that a person below the age of eighteen is no longer liable for the death sentence. Prior to this enactment it was not unusual for persons as young as sixteen to be sentenced to death.

It is also important to note that the Court pointed out that the United States was at variance with the ideas of justice of many countries it was wont to compare itself with. That America's Supreme Court should have remarked on this raises the hope that, as the country is beginning to find itself increasingly alone among the democracies in matters relating to the death penalty, we may see a change in the not too distant future. It is to be hoped that, in the long term, viewing the death penalty in the light of other countries' legislation may induce the Supreme Court to prohibit it as 'cruel or unusual'. Failing that, we can only hope that an increasing number of states will follow the example of Maryland, which, at the time of writing (2014), is the latest of them to do away with the death penalty, which it did in 2013.

The story of Ivan Ray Murphy Jr is, as I have said, the story of a human being. But it also illustrates why Amnesty International firmly believes that the death penalty is a contravention of human rights. The official interpretation of human rights does not totally prohibit execution, though various UN organs have repeatedly affirmed that it is the organization's aim that the world should eventually end executions altogether. Despite this, it accepts that the death penalty may be imposed for the 'gravest' crimes.

We in Amnesty find this hard to comprehend. We base our view mainly on Article 5 of the Universal Declaration of Human Rights, which is further enlarged upon in the International Covenant on Civil and Political Rights and the Convention against Torture and Other Cruel, Inhuman or Degrading Treatment or Punishment.

After reading the story of Ivan Ray Murphy's last hours, I can but conclude that the procedure leading up to an execution can only be described as cruel and inhuman.

NOTES

[1] 'Murphy trial underway', *The Denison Herald* (16.10.1990).

[2] 'Murder trial begins Monday', *Sherman Democrat* (14.10.1990).

[3] 'Murphy transferred to Grayson jail', *The Denison Herald* (1.10.1989).

[4] 'Final arguments next up in Murphy murder trial', *Sherman Democrat* (25.10.1990).

[5] 'Murder trial begins Monday', *Sherman Democrat* (14.10.1990).

[6] 'Stuff case heads to grand jury', *The Denison Herald* (28.10.1990).

[7] 'Potts refuses testimony', *The Denison Herald* (24.10.1990).

[8] Negotiations during a criminal trial in which the accused agrees to admit to a lesser crime in exchange for which the prosecutor agrees to ask for a more lenient sentence than would have been recommended if the original charge had been proceeded with. In a case involving, for example, murder, the defence may submit a plea for the defendant to be charged with unintentional rather than intentional (wilful) murder. In US law this is known as 'plea bargaining'.

[9] For further information see http://www.judiciary.senate.gov/hearings

[10] Statistics from 'Death Penalty Representation'. For further information see http://www.deathpenaltyinfo.org/death-penalty-representation

[11] Quoted from 'Death Penalty News & Updates', available on http://people.smu.edu/rhalperi/

[12] See http://deathpenaltyinfo.org/national-polls-and-studies

[13] Quoted from 'Death Penalty News & Updates', available from http://people.smu.edu/rhalperi/

[14] Writ of Certiorari. For further information see http://en.wikipedia.org/wiki/Certiorari

[15] Quoted from 'Death Penalty News and Updates', available from http://people.smu.edu/rhalperi/

[16] Still active as a guest house for the families of inmates. www.thehospitalityhouse.org

[17] All prisoners under sentence of death in Texas are handcuffed when not in their cells. See 'Prison conditions for death row and life without parole inmates' at http://www.cga.ct.gov/2011/rpt/2011-R-0178.htm

[18] 'Texas Coalition to Abolish the Death Penalty'. See http://www.aclutx.org/strategic-campaigns/criminal-law-reform/death-penalty/

[19] There have been a few occasions when condemned prisoners have themselves elected to be executed by electric chair. The last such instance was in January 2013, when Robert Gleason Jr chose this method; most prisoners opt for poison, however. In the past, three different drugs were employed: the first to put the prisoner to sleep, the second to stop breathing and the third to stop the heart. Nowadays, most states use only one drug, pentobarbital. According to the Norwegian branch of Amnesty International, pharmaceutical companies in the United States and elsewhere have in recent years done their best to ensure that their products are not used for executions. This has led to a shortage of pentobarbital for this purpose, with the result that some states have been forced to suspend executions while others have had recourse to different drugs. There have been cases when this has led to mishaps, as in Oklahoma in 2014 when Clayton Lockett died of heart failure while being executed

[20] See 'Death Penalty Costs in Texas Outweigh Life Imprisonment' on the website http://deathpenalty-info-org/costs-death-penalty-costs.texas-outweigh -life-imprisonment

[21] For Judge Baird's letter of dissent, see http://www.leagle,com/decision/1996945917SW2d28_1935. Baird stands out in Texas as being the only judge to have exonerated, in retrospect, a man (Tim Cole) who had died a natural death in prison. For further information, see http://en.wikikipedia.org/wiki/charlie_baird

22   Figures quoted from 'Death Penalty News &
     Updates', available on http://people.smu.edu/rhalperi/
23   Figures quoted from 'Death Penalty News &
     Updates', available on http://people.smu.edu/rhalperi/
24   In 1984, Velma Barfield was executed in North
     Carolina.
25   Figures quoted from 'Death Penalty News &
     Updates', available on http://people.smu.edu/rhalperi/
26   See Robert Excell White' on
     http://murderpedia.org/male.W/w1/white-robert-
     excell.htm
27   At the time of writing, on average prisoners under
     sentence of death spend a total of eight years on
     Death Row. Source: 'Death Penalty News &
     Updates', available on http://people.smu.edu/rhalperi/
28   Timothy McVeigh's bombing in Oklahoma City in
     1995 left 168 people dead and more than 680 injured.
     In consequence, the right of people sentenced to
     death to appeal was curtailed when the Antiterrorism
     and Effective Death Penalty Act came into force in
     the spring of 1996. McVeigh was executed six years
     later, on 11 June 2001. However, as the new law was
     not made retroactive, it did not affect Pee-Wee. For
     further details, see
     http://en.wikipedia.org/wiki/Antiterrorism_and_
     Effextive_Death_Penalty_Act_of_1996
     A summary of the text is available on
     www.fas.org/irp/crs/96-499.htm
29   Michael Dewayne Johnson took his own life in his
     cell on 19 October 2006, 15 hours before he was due
     to be executed. For further details see
     http://murderpedia.org/male.J/j/johnson-michael-
     dewayne.htm Figures quoted from 'Death Penalty
     News & Updates' available on
     http://people.smu.edu/rhalperi/
30   Figures quoted from 'Death Penalty News &
     Updates', available on http://people.smu.edu/rhalperi/
31   The first execution under the new law took place in
     1977.
32   There have been a number of incidents involving
     misuse of pepper sprays in American prisons. See,
     for example, 'Horrific Pepper Spray Videos Force

Change in California', *Huffington Post* (24.1.2013), available on http://wwww.huffingtonpost.com/2013/10/24/calif-prisons-pepper-spray-mentally-ill_n_4158467.html

33   Since 2011, prisoners scheduled for execution in Texas have no longer been allowed to choose what they would like for their last meal. See 'Texas Prisons End Last Meal Tradition on Death Row' *Time* (23.09.2011), available on http://newsfeed.time.com/2011/09/23/texas-prisons-end-last-meal-tradition-on-death-row/

34   The man concerned was Odell Barnes. However, despite support from abroad, Barnes was executed on

1   March 2000. He made a name for himself by requesting for his last meal 'justice, equality and world peace'. See http://murderpedia.org/male.B/b1/barnes-odell.htm

35   When it was opened in November 1993, the Polunsky Unit was known as the Terrell Unit. At that time, the general public did not associate the name with a prison for men under sentence of death, as all the inmates in that category were then on Death Row in Ellis Unit. But when they were transferred to the new prison, the prison was renamed Polunsky because the man it had originally been named after, Charles T. Terrell, resented being associated with a prison housing men condemned to die. See http://en.wikipedia.org/wiki/Allan_B._Polunsky_Unit

36   Figures taken from 'Death Penalty News & Updates', available on http://people.smu.edu/rhalperi/

37   Figures taken from 'Death Penalty News & Updates', available on http://people.smu.edu/rhalperi/

38   See www.innocenceproject.org

39   Figures taken from 'Death Penalty News & Updates', available on http://people.smu.edu/rhalperi/

40   'Ivan Ray Murphy Jr.' on Murderpedia, The Encyclopedia of Murderers. See http://murderpedia.org/male.M/m1/murphy-ivan-ray.htm

41   'Figures taken from 'Death Penalty News & Updates', available on http://people.smu.edu/rhalperi

42	Since this was written, with the help of Pee-Wee's sister I have traced Pee-Wee's ex-wife but, to my regret, I have been unable establish contact with either her or his daughter.
43	I have this update from Heidi Vindenes, who corresponded with a prisoner on Death Row in the unit. Such transfers can be a mixed blessing, as they mean the prisoners afterwards tend to receive fewer visitors and are thus more isolated than ever.
44	Information from Jon Trana, Amnesty International Norway.
45	See www.jpay.com
46	See http://en.wikipedia.org/wiki/Gary_Gilmore
47	No executions took place in the US in1978, but between 1979 and 1983 ten people were put to death there.The number of executions has subsequently climbed steadily.
48	All figures quoted in the Epilogue are from Rick Halperin's 'Death Penalty News & Updates', available on http://people.smu.edu/rhalperi/
49	See 'Death Sentences and Executions 2013. Amnesty International, March 2014, available on http://www.amnestyusa.org/sites/default/files/act500 012014en.pdf
50	http://www.pewresearch.org./fact-tank/2014/02/12support-for-death-penalty-drops-among-americans/
51	See http://en.wikipedia.org/wiki/All-white_jury
52	Augustsson, Lars-Åke (2004): *Nära döden. Om dödsstraffet, Texas, USA – och om oss*, Leopard förlag, p. 94. See also http://en.wikipedia.org/wiki/Jury_selection
53	See 'Louisiana's longest-serving death row prisoner walks free after 30 years' (CNN 12 March 2014), available on http://edition.cnn.com/2014/03/11/us/louisiana-glenn-ford-freed/